MOC HOA

(mŏck wauh)

A Vietnam Medical-Military Adventure

Larry P. Kammholz, M.D.

Best wishes

Published by:
    Starboard Publishing
    Oshkosh, Wisconsin 54901   U.S.A.

Printed in the United States of America
    Castle-Pierce Press, Oshkosh, WI

Publishing Date 1990

Publisher's Cataloging Information
    Kammholz, Larry P., M.D.
    MOC HOA
    A Vietnam Medical-Military Adventure
    Non-Fiction

Library of Congress Catalog Card Number 89 - 91084

ISBN   0-9622696-4-6   Softcover

ISBN 0-9622696-4-6
MOC HOA

To

Those I knew in Vietnam

ARTIST'S FOREWORD

Doing the artwork for Moc Hoa was a joy for me. There will be millions of words printed about Vietnam. Movies, books, TV shows, etc. are already pouring into the industry of commerce and profit. Some works are good. Some are great. The joy of Moc Hoa is that it's great and it's "haunting." It's great because of Dr. Kammholz's honesty and sincerity. It's "haunting" because it's Vietnam in an intensely-concentrated, tense, and all-encompassing exposure. The action takes place in a medical setting but the truths are universal. To tell a haunting story full of universal truths is the essence of literature.

From an artistic standpoint I can see Moc Hoa as a healing square of white with a red cross set into a vast blue area of water and green place of jungle. And it's concentrated there, squeezed into there, and busy there. If you went to Vietnam, you were always squeezed into someplace and you were always busy — sometimes doing anything to avoid loneliness and thinking about where you were. In this case of Moc Hoa, the business was fast and furious. You feel a doctor trying to heal a massive wound — working with dedication and belief. And the great thing about the book is that you feel and know he did the best he could — even if the biggest patient — Vietnam — could not be saved. You know this and you feel good. You feel good, especially if you are a Vietnam veteran; you shared the doctor's struggle — in your own way — to make the country well. You feel good because the honesty of the doctor is your honesty — his struggle yours and his victory, in spite of ultimate defeat — your victory.

Dr. Kammholz changes colors into words and adds a haunting quality to his painting which few artists can do.

Theodore William Gostas
Combat Artist
POW Vietnam — 1968-1973
Major, U.S. Army (Retired)

Sept. 6, 1988
Cheyenne, Wyoming

ACKNOWLEDGMENTS

I wish to thank my daughter Jodi Kammholz for her help in reviewing and improving the text. I also wish to thank my son-in-law, Tim Gerritsen, for his help and comments, and production of the maps. To Ruth and Ray Burger, my aunt and uncle, I express my appreciation for the safekeeping of my letters until I returned. I wish to recognize the Fox Valley Vietnam Veterans' Association and Ron Sager. Ron reviewed the work, and it was through him and the association that I met the artist, Ted Gostas, to whom I owe my special thanks. Finally, I wish to thank my wife Bonnie, my mother Esther, and my children Heidi and Craig, for their understanding and encouragement.

AUTHOR'S PREFACE

The story takes place in the Mekong Delta in a province bordering Cambodia. It was a scene of scattered Special Forces camps with their Vietnamese Irregular supporting troops. One-third of the population of Moc Hoa consisted of refugees from North Vietnam who had come to the South after the division of the country.

The time of this story extends from the summer of 1966 until I left in mid-1967 and then continues with information from letters I received afterward until ''Tet'' some months later. I was drafted just after finishing internship. It was somewhat early in the war and large units of U.S. forces were beginning to enter the country.

The ''Pacification'' effort was being pushed and our MILPHAP (Military Provincial Hospital Assistance Program) team was a part of this effort. We were more under the jurisdiction of USAID (United States Agency for International Development) than we were the military, although we were all military personnel. We were to support and help train the Vietnamese in the province hospital. It would be important to maintain good relationships with our Vietnamese counterparts. Later our mission was to extend our men to help at health clinics in outlying areas of the province to push rural health and the pacification effort.

The bulk of this text was written shortly after events occurred in Vietnam. Although some parts were expanded upon later, most remains as it was originally written. A few sections — the Fort Sam Houston episodes, ''A Process of Evil,'' the last paragraph of ''One-Eyed Bird,'' and some others were written at a later date.

The artist, Theodore Gostas, was captured in Hue during the Tet offensive and was to spend the next five years as a prisoner of war, much of it in the jungle. He underwent great physical and mental torment, and was fortunate to have survived.

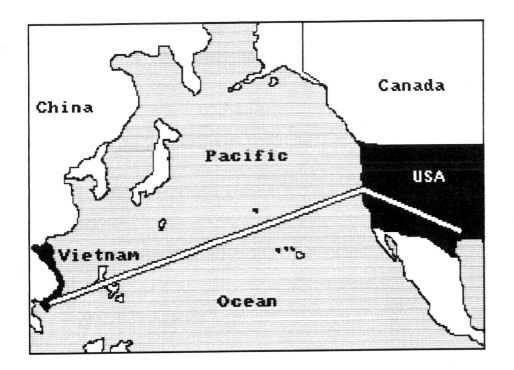 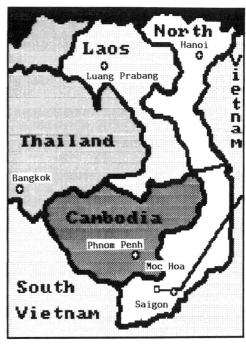

It was a typical 95 degree San Antonio summer day when I arrived at Fort "Sam." I had been assigned to a MILPHAP (Military Provincial Hospital Assistance Program) team, consisting of three M.D.'s and 12 enlisted men. Our duty would be to supplement Vietnamese civilian care in a Vietnamese hospital. Fifteen such groups had preceded us. Three weeks of instruction followed with training in things such as tropical diseases, tooth extraction, ether anesthesia and battle injuries. The team was to have what I thought was a good deal of equipment including two generators, two jeeps, pharmaceuticals, some surgical instruments and a set-up for a small medical lab and X-ray unit.

From San Antonio we were flown, strapped in backwards, in a huge new C-5A Galaxy transport jet [see picture 33-a, page 33] which stopped in the dead of night at a base near San Francisco. There we sat for a while refueling. Then we took off again. It was not a time of conversation. After many hours, the darkness gave way to daylight. The senses noted mainly the sunlit metallic aluminum of the interior and the hushed whishing and whistling sounds as the jet passed through the high atmosphere. The flight stretched on much longer than I had thought and we were numbed into a state of unremitting grogginess. It went on and on and seemed to be almost unending. Then suddenly we banked and went down — down into Tan Son Nhut.

We disembarked and on wobbly legs walked a short way to the terminal and were given a few short briefings by U.S. people. Then we were all taken to a room where we were asked by Vietnamese airport personnel if we had brought anything with us which was not permitted. We had earlier been told to remember that we were there on the invitation of the Vietnamese people. Guns were not permitted in Saigon for the safety of the Vietnamese people. We would be issued weapons just before leaving Saigon for our permanent location. Practically all of the men in our new unit had purchased a handgun in Texas. I had not liked the accuracy of the Army .45s and bought a .38 special with holster and a .22 Barretta automatic. My safety was important to me, too. If they were going to invite us to such a place, it seemed reasonable to have something with which to defend ourselves. So we kept our mouths shut and hung on to our weapons.

TAXI RIDE

From Tan Son Nhut we were bussed to the Koepler Hotel. The next day, late in the afternoon, I had gone back to the airport to try and get the rest of my baggage. Two of my men had gone with me, but I wound up having to get back to the hotel alone. They had ditched me, I think on purpose, to have some excitement. Anyway, I hailed a taxi — a stick-shift Volkswagen Beetle — and got in the back. It was dark out. The driver didn't seem to understand much English and I showed him a slip of paper with the name and address of the hotel to which he was to take me. I pronounced the name of the hotel and he seemed to understand, so off we went. After we drove some distance, I began wondering if it might be possible that rather than heading to the hotel, I was instead being taken to the outskirts. In these circumstances I figured I was a pretty good candidate for being set up to be ambushed. As the cab jerked along I leaned forward and quietly opened the duffel bag on the floor. I reached in and placed my hand on the handle of my revolver. My uneasiness with the situation was transmitted to the taxi driver who I'm sure must have sensed that I was up to something. Here we were, me in the back on the edge of my seat and the driver on edge because of my nervousness. This in a way was OK, I thought, because he would be less likely to pull a fast one. Many blocks we went in this way, with dim yellow and red neon here and there lighting up in the streets the silhouettes of Asian clad apparitions. Finally we arrived at the hotel. I'm sure the cabbie was as glad to be rid of me as I was to be out of his cab. There had been no ambush and I had made it back alone.

THE KOEPLER

For the next few weeks the team was housed at the Koepler Hotel. This was a chalky white building of about eight stories with unenclosed windows. The stairway up the side was exposed in places to sniper fire so we used the elevator instead. It was a rickety elevator with a metal scissors gate for a door. If you stuck your arm through the gate when the elevator was moving, you could easily lose that arm. I'd been on old elevators like this before in some old buildings in Chicago and Milwaukee and particularly the old Sears store in Fond du Lac, Wisconsin. I had worked there as a stockboy when I was in high school. I'd haul mattresses and box springs from the basement receiving room to the top floor storage. The Sears and Koepler elevators were of the same caliber. They

didn't go fast, but every half floor or so there would be irregular jerkings and squealings from the cable. What went through your mind was that, with the way the elevator sounded, the cable might slip off or break at any moment and down the shaft it would go with you watching the floors zip by. Down you would go to a smashing landing at the bottom. If still alive, you could look back up and watch for the rest of the cable parts to come crashing through the roof and finish you off. Enough about the elevator.

On the ground floor of the Koepler was a rather pleasant small eating area where we would sometimes spend hours discussing plans and the daily events. At the start we felt safer in the Koepler than we did on the street, even though the back of the Brinks Hotel had been bombed out a few weeks earlier. There were briefings to go to in other parts of the city and we used military busses to get around town. As the days passed, we felt increasingly at ease in the streets but still tried to remain on guard. We might hop on a bus and drive for half an hour through the traffic [33-c] to a meeting at the USAID house. Other days we'd drive a similar distance to a meeting at Tan Son Nhut. Sometimes we'd take pedicabs [33-d] and once I paid for a ride with a businessman on the back of his motorscooter. Some of the enlisted men visited other men with jobs like theirs in the local military hospitals. They figured this might come in handy for future scrounging expeditions or as just a way to make contacts in Saigon. I'd go for meals with our officers to the Brinks and at times I'd go with some of our enlisted men to the Hoa Loo which was only one-half block away from the Koepler. The Hoa Loo was an enlisted men's hotel. While eating there we were entertained by a Vietnamese rock band which wasn't half bad. They'd play morale boosting songs such as, "My Bonnie Lies Over the Ocean" (my wife's name is Bonnie) and "Take me home...to the place...I was born." I wondered if maybe they were being paid by a VC psychological warfare committee.

15 July 1966

This is the fourth day in Saigon. As I write this I am on the top bunk of room 511 in the Koepler [33-e] and can see the afternoon rain clouds approaching — grey thunderheads in an otherwise entire grey overcast. This is the third day of rain about this time in the afternoon. Jerry F., a few others of the team, and I took a military bus to attend a briefing on the Fourth Corps area. Jerry is the other doctor on our team. The captain giving the briefing had not seen Moc Hoa, our duty assignment. Moc Hoa is the chief town of Kien Tuong Province. It is 60 miles west of Saigon in the Plain of Reeds, four miles from the Cambodian border. During the wet season most of the land is supposedly under eight feet of water with elephant grass protruding six feet above the water level. I can't quite believe this. The province is the most sparsely populated of the Delta provinces. It is considered to be the Siberia of Vietnam. It certainly doesn't sound as though living in this area is going to be easy.

THE MARSH

I was used to swamps. The town I grew up in was located at the foot of the largest lake in the state on the southern end of which was a big cattail marsh. As a boy, I would often bike there in the spring to go fishing with my friends. We would put on our hip boots and wade through the marsh. If we weren't careful, the water could go over the top of the boots. We'd go 100 yards through thigh-deep water to get to the cinder track. This was part of an old railroad bed. Then we'd go along this for another 50 yards to the other side of the bank where the fishing was better and there were few fishermen. We'd wade several yards out to the edge of the cattails and set out our poles. There were crappies, bullheads and northern pike. I had one favorite spot and if I fished out from it, I'd practically always come back home with some good-sized pike on my stringer. I'd put a minnow on with a steel leader and cork and I'd often use a fly rod. It was fun fighting the pike but a bit tricky bringing him into the net while avoiding the weeds and at the same time not sinking too deep in the muck. These were idyllic spring days of adventure spent watching a bobber and enjoying the warm sun amidst the cattails and reeds. So I was no stranger to a swamp and had spent many an enjoyable day in Soupley's Marsh, Lake Winnebago, Fond du Lac, Wisconsin.

15 July 1966 continued

Mac, our pharmacist, has been at the 17th Field Hospital obtaining supplies again. Apparently some of our pharmaceuticals didn't arrive in the amount we were supposed to get. We are, of course, not authorized to obtain supplies from this source, but Mac knows the 17th's pharmacist and a few others there and today obtained more antibiotics. He already has three briefcases of medicine. This should help when we get started. I can't imagine trying to practice medicine without antibiotics. Jerry and I have decided to avoid, if we can, obtaining supplies by Mac's method, but if we find that necessary supplies are impossible to come by and plentiful elsewhere, then we shall let Mac do his trading.

One of the Vietnamese girls in the cafeteria today said, "You numba one" and showed me a tube of lipstick. Apparently this was a suggestion that I should bring her some lipstick from the PX or food service wouldn't be so hot anymore.

Saigon street scenes.

Our MSC officer, Bill R., just arrived from Moc Hoa with a report on the situation — much better than we anticipated. We are to be at a 70-bed hospital. A young Vietnamese doctor who speaks English is presently there. The town numbers about 7,000 with 50 Special Forces personnel. There hasn't been the amount of water in the region as described in the briefing for three years. Jerry and I spent the rest of the evening going over a written description of the facilities and general health situation in the region. One of the waitresses and a hotel boy who happened to be in the cafeteria seemed quite interested in the pamphlet we were reading. We wondered if they might be VC plants.

Saigon street scene.

16 July

We spent most of the morning getting some of our baggage at Tan Son Nhut airport. In the afternoon, Jerry, Bill and I went to the Brinks Hotel [33-b] for lunch and then looked around a bit in downtown Saigon. The streets were filled with vendors selling clothing, hardware and handicrafts. I purchased a string and bow type musical instrument having a gourd-sounding base. I also purchased a Chinese outfit for my daughter, Jodi, and a housecoat for my wife, Bonnie. The vendor asked 400 p's (piasters) for the housecoat and we finally agreed on 200. Back at the Koepler, the Vietnamese women at the desk told me that the musical instrument was a good buy, but that I had paid three times what the housecoat was worth and that the material was of poor quality.

I went to the Brinks Hotel with Sergeant Brown and Jerry for lunch and spent the rest of the afternoon downtown. We walked five blocks down to the Saigon River [33-g, h] and back. We stopped in a cafe and had some Vietnamese beer — not much different from beer in the States and better than Texas beer. Brown told us he saw an American carrying beer from the PX into a local tavern by the case — the black market. Along the streets one is frequently stopped and asked to change scrip for p's. They have means of changing scrip into dollars which are then used by the Communist bloc, so we are told. As I am writing this in the Koepler, I heard about ten gunshots out on the street. None of the others in the room seemed disturbed that this might be a prelude to bombing of the hotel. They said they would expect much more racket. Anyway, I got down off the top bunk. This was about 10 p.m. and I told myself to hereafter be in before dark.

Pedicab.

18 July

I spent some of the day downtown again, mainly taking pictures. Ed A., a fellow M.D. from Fort Eustis, invited Jerry and me for dinner at his villa. Ed is with the 17th Field Hospital in Saigon. He volunteered for duty here four months ago in hopes of being assigned to the 17th Field and in hopes of finishing his tour of duty here that much earlier. We took a cab to the Metropole Hotel which is across from the 17th Field and met Ed there and then drove to the villa. This was located next to the main Buddhist temple where there had been a good deal of action on the street during the Buddhist riots. The villa itself was secure, however, for also adjacent to it was a housing area for ARVIN troops.

Ed had two housegirls who did the cooking and the laundry. They served a Vietnamese dinner with soup, rice and pineapple, rice and beef, tough chicken sliced like bread, bananas and a green vegetable which looked like four-inch lengths of green straw. All of the meal, except for the chicken, was tasty.

We discussed a number of interesting subjects that evening. Ed felt that the rate of exchange of scrip for p's was quite unfair to Americans, for the true rate of exchange should be more nearly $1 for 200 p's and many American personnel thus exchange money with the local populace rather than at the exchange centers. Ed related that Jim Hay, another one of the M.D.'s from Fort Eustis, was located at Bien Hoa, which is ten miles north of Saigon. His unit was staying in tents and the area is all red clay. A young engineer, Pete B., dropped in. His reasons for being in Vietnam were apparently money and excitement. Pete spoke Vietnamese well and taught us to say a few things. One of Ed's fellow M.D.'s showed slides and movies of Saigon. Pete offered to drive us back and gave us an evening tour of Saigon in his Volkswagen. This I didn't particularly appreciate from a safety standpoint.

19 July

Today we were taken to the Ministry of Health and given briefings by the administrative personnel who will handle the Fourth Corps area. The briefing included a discussion of the supply system which is not working well at present. The Navy team that came with us will be receiving six U.S. nurses. The Air Force and our team will have no U.S. nurses because of the security problem in our areas. We were informed of a $100 a month fund that we have for miscellaneous use for hospital improvements, however, the paperwork sounds so involved that it must have been set up in order to curtail use of the fund.

We heard today that the VC have stolen 1,500 lbs. of plastic explosive in Saigon and they have openly sent threats to four hotels that they may be bombed tonight. They purportedly gave a priority list: A hotel housing MP's being number one, the Hoa Loo (one-half block from here), number two, and the Koepler, number four.

Last night the guards woke everyone on the first and second floors and had them place their steel helmets by their beds. If we hear what appears to be an attack outside, we are to roll out of bed, put on our steel helmets and cover ourselves with the mattress to minimize blast effects. The threat for tonight is because today is the anniversary of the division of Vietnam into North and South.

20 July

Nothing was bombed last night, though at 10 p.m. a shot went off in the hotel — probably someone loading his gun. I spent most of the evening in the Koepler cafeteria and met Major Dan T. of the Medical Service Corps. He is to be in charge of medical evacuation flights to Japan and the U.S. At this time there are a number of good U.S. hospitals in Japan which are not being utilized. Most of the seriously injured troops are evacuated to the States. He is going to divert some of these to Japan — a shorter flight and just as adequate facilities as in the U.S.

Among other things he told us of a practice that some higher ranking servicemen in Japan have. They fly to Vietnam for the last and first day of the month and collect $200 for Vietnam duty for those two months. The major also described Tokyo as a good place for leave and told me that I should try to get there. He offered to arrange accommodation for me on a med. evac. flight to Tokyo.

They have been firing flares and artillery tonight to the north of Saigon, which one can see quite well from the fifth floor here [33-f].

22 July

THE SNIPER

At 10 a.m. today I was standing in the hall on the fifth floor of the Koepler when three shots rang out. It sounded as if they may have come from the floor above me. One of the maids ran up to the sixth floor to look. The people on the block immediately ran out of their shops and one of the MP guards at the front gate ran around to the alley. The people on the street level said that someone had seen a sniper on one of the rooftops behind the hotel. After 10 minutes of searching, a man was captured. He was an old, bearded man, all dressed in white. I believe it is the custom to be dressed in white at one's funeral. Probably some younger VC talked this old man into this, he perhaps not having long to live at his age. So he dressed himself up in his funeral whites and went out to shoot some Americans. There also had been reports of some sniping in the downtown area last night. Jerry and I decided to cancel our excursions for the day.

THE BAR

We're still sitting in Saigon waiting for transportation to Moc Hoa. Two of our men were in a bar fight last night. Three from the other teams and the two from ours went down to the Puerto Rican bar, which is one block from the Koepler. They were sitting at the bar and a Vietnamese nudged one of the Air Force men in the back. He ignored this, but the man hit him three more times so the fourth time, he turned and slugged the Vietnamese in the teeth, knocking him across the room and tearing a gash in his ear. Thereupon ten Vietnamese got up and started for the Air Force man. The five Americans grabbed beer bottles and began backing out of the bar. The Vietnamese followed; one — a ranger — had a heavy piece of pipe. This one and two others came at the five U.S. guys and were slugged with the beer bottles. At that point the MP's showed up and the fight was over. I told our guys to stay the hell out of fights from now on or we'd restrict them to the hotel.

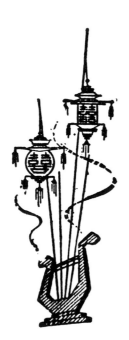

RICE KRISPIES

We're in the Koepler, anxious to get going to Moc Hoa and the waiting is getting long.

As I sit here I can think back to Medical Field Service School at Fort Sam Houston in San Antonio, Texas. There wasn't room in the barracks so officers were given a certain amount of money to rent another place to stay. At first I had a pretty good one-story motel with a nice pool. I usually had the pool to myself after dusk. One end was deep and had a diving board and the water was always warmed from the heat of the day.

After two weeks I thought I'd save some money, so I moved to an older motel where each room had a small kitchen. The first night, about 20 minutes after I turned out the lights, I became vaguely aware of an undefinable presence in the room. I tried to get to sleep but the vague sensation of something going on in the room continued. It sounded like a bowl of Rice Krispies. After a few more minutes of this, I sat up and turned on the light. In front of me I beheld 70 or 80 Texas-sized cockroaches flicking their antennae and crawling on the counter and over the floor. It was late and I risked not finding another place to stay, but I bugged out of there and found another motel — minus Texas cockroaches.

TEXAS AMBUSH

Basic training included classes in preventive medicine, tropical medicine, battle injuries, tooth extractions and many other things. At one point goats were shot and killed and we practiced debriding (surgically removing dead tissue) the wounds. We practiced doing cricothyroidotomies. This is a quick incision into the trachea of the neck to produce an airway.

Every day there was marching. Lots of it. There were field exercises which were more interesting. One day they told us we were going to practice what to do in case of an ambush. We were taken on trucks and given directions that when we came to a halt, we were to get out and, as quickly as possible, throw ourselves down to the side of the road. We loaded into the trucks which had canvas covers, side benches and an open back. The day was hot, nearly

100 degrees. We were driven quite a way out and then off and down a dusty road into some low hills. Dust billowed into the back of the truck as we were jostled and bounced about. The truck moved slower for a while, then suddenly stopped and we scrambled out. I ran to the side of the road and threw myself to the ground. Up flew red-brown dust which gritted in my teeth, but quickly my attention was directed elsewhere. Sharp needle-like pain came jabbing into me. I tried to hold still. If I moved there was more pain, and we weren't supposed to get up until the all-clear was given. Flat Texas cactus had been lying there, concealed from my quick glance. The organizers of all this had planned their ambush well. I had learned a lesson in following directions and I'd keep it in mind for the next event.

WHATEVER ELSE

They hauled us out of San Antonio again, this time to Camp Bullis, which is big Texas range country. There were large tents, K-rations, excursions of various kinds. One day our preventive medicine field exercise was to locate and identify some scorpions, black widows, brown spiders and whatever else we could find. In the morning we marched down the road to a mound covered with knee-high grass. There we were told to stand up on the mound and were given a prolonged talk. The next day we knew why. We had found our scorpions and spiders and up on the mound "whatever else" (chiggers) had crawled up to the top of our ankles to the elastic boot band. There they stopped and decided to have a meal. We all wound up with a batch of fluid-filled blisters that itched like mad. Scratching them only made things worse. If you carefully popped the blisters and gently expressed the fluid without getting it into the tissue around it, you could get some relief. We had been bushwhacked. From thenceforth we would always have sympathy for troops with chigger bites.

THE REDSKIN

The marching back at Fort Sam was not always dull. Our company leader, Captain S., was a thin M.D. with a high-pitched, somewhat sissified voice. A couple of men toward the back of the column had been in the habit of heckling him during the marching. He couldn't tell who they were, so he decided to take it out on the whole company. The routine of marching was for us to go a reasonably good number of paces before another order was given. Now, he called out orders in rapid succession. It was three steps forward and "to the rear march," and four steps more and "by the right flank march" and so forth. Fortunately, he didn't keep this up long. I think he sensed he was starting to push his luck. The men in the rear set about planning their revenge and a few days later Camp Bullis provided the chance.

One night while he was sleeping, five or six of the men crept up to his bunk. They grabbed his arms and legs and, holding him by all fours, proceeded down to the small reservoir and pitched him in, over the deep end of the dam. Some time went by and then he came back, covered with the red-brown mud of the reservoir bank, sneaking into camp as though he were an Indian from another era. So, one good thing had happened at Camp Bullis and marching reverted back to dullness.

TEXAS RAIN

We were back at Fort Sam having classes. Apparently the powers in charge had been waiting for a certain type of weather forecast. Unexpectedly, we were bussed out about 20 miles to a spot to set up camp. There was a steady rain on the way, not a common occurrence in this part of Texas. Once there, we got out of the busses and trudged some distance to the campsite, which was under water. We were told to pick out a tent site anyway, to be ready when the water went down. The rain continued and we were kept there for a long time. Finally, we were herded back into the busses and driven out, but, a mile down the road, the bus came to a halt. Those in the front of the bus were getting off so the rest of us got up and went out, too. There, a short way in front, a flash flood had cut off the road we had come in on. The water was as high as the top of a car and about 50 yards wide. Large branches and dead trees rode by swiftly. We stood there and watched this for a while and then were herded back into the bus and taken on a long detour in the opposite direction. We thought for sure we were going to get cut off by another flood, but that didn't happen. If they would have done this a little differently, maybe there would have been headlines reading, "Army Doctors Drowned in Flash Flood."

WHERE THE DEER AND THE ANTELOPE PLAY

We were at Camp Bullis again. It was the timed, night compass course and we were assembled in teams of three. I hadn't known the other two on my team but they knew each other. One was a wiry, red-headed, freckled fellow from Missouri who didn't act like he wanted to be very friendly, but wanted to run the show. The other guy went along with whatever he said. Each team had its own compass setting. Some miles out we were to run into a fence line on different points of which were posted coordinates for each team to follow to get back to the busses. We'd have only a few hours to make it back. If we didn't, we would be spending the night out on the range with the deer and the rattlesnakes.

One of us would go about 100 yards ahead. We'd wave him to one side or the other to line him up with the coordinates. Then he'd stay in position until we arrived. Then we'd repeat the process. This was accurate, but it soon became clear that it was going to be too slow, and increasing darkness was making everything more difficult. Our freckled teammate got the idea that we should pick out a star on the coordinate line and follow it. This was a good idea and we now could move along at a fast clip. We came to the fence line and 50 yards down it found our new coordinates. As we headed back, the terrain was more open and we could travel even faster. The other two started picking up the pace. It was evident they were up to something. I wasn't about to let them have the satisfaction of ditching me. There were open patches with sparse grass, dead branches, rocks and scattered scrub trees. Stumbling over objects came unpredictably. We scrambled through a ravine, tripping over rocks and, sometimes, falling headlong into the dirt. At one point I was startled to see the outline of a longhorn standing 20 yards off to the side, watching us. I thought cattle slept lying down. We must have awakened him. I wondered if next I'd come across a rattlesnake. The other two didn't slacken the half-trotting, stumbling pace. To their displeasure I kept up. I had been athletic in high school and I wasn't going to get beat at this game.

We made it to the bus and on time. I could hardly believe a few of the other teams were there already. Maybe they had a shorter route or didn't start as slowly as us. More teams straggled in over the next half hour. Then, the bus took off — on schedule — as we were told, and ours wasn't one of the teams that spent the night out on the range.

DARTS

One afternoon there was a weapons demonstration. Mortars and machine guns were demonstrated. We pulled pins on dud grenades and threw them. We fired different types of rifles. I was impressed with the BAR (Browning Automatic Rifle of WW II). It threw a heavy slug way out a good distance. The amount of dirt it kicked up impressed me. On another day they put us through the obstacle course. We had to crawl through barbed wire, dragging on our stomaches, with live machine-gun rounds and tracers flying four to six feet over our heads.

We all knew about the build-up in Vietnam, but figured that those who got assigned to U.S. places would have a better chance of not being sent over. One day as we were standing at ease in formation, one of the younger M.D. instructors called out the names of about 20 of us and told us to come over to where he was standing. There we were told that we had been picked from the group to stay for the preventive medicine course. When I heard this, I realized that it was certain that I was going to be sent to Vietnam. Then, there came upon me a feeling of numbness accompanied by an almost paralysis of movement. I was in for it and I knew it. Later, the rumor was that they had picked us by throwing darts at the roster sheet. Wherever the dart hit, the next five men down were chosen for the course. Then they'd throw the dart again and, "where it lands, nobody knows!" Fair as anything else, I suppose…

MOC HOA

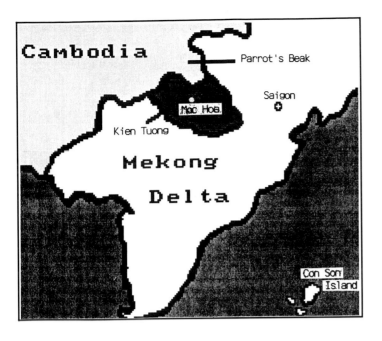

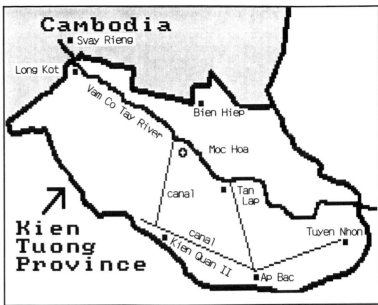

25 July [34-a, c]

We flew into Moc Hoa in a Caribou. It is a 25-minute flight from Saigon. The town is much cleaner than Saigon. In certain ways, it is somewhat like a small U.S. country town. There are a few Special Forces personnel here and a number of different Vietnamese units, so that security should be halfway decent. There are 7,000 people in the town, 30 percent of whom are Catholic refugees who came when the country was divided in 1956. The main compound of the Special Forces B-Team [34-b, d, e, f] is about one-quarter of a block in size. Here is where our enlisted men are staying. Bill, Jerry and I are staying at the home of the USAID representative. It is a two-story, cement building and fairly comfortable. We are six blocks from the compound and I feel somewhat ill-at-ease about this.

The personnel from the hospital and outlying district health personnel were gathered in front of the hospital [35-a] to meet us. The Vietnamese doctor, Dr. Ting [53-f, g], speaks English fairly well. He's about my age. Later, we were invited to attend the Special Forces briefings on operations in the area. The first one was very interesting and I shall attempt to attend as many of these as possible. That first night we were awakened at 3 a.m. We were told that one of the Special Forces' interpreters had been shot through the hip with a .45. This happened in an argu-

ment over a girl. We found out later that the woman was married and that she and the interpreter had become involved. The woman's husband got wind of it and checked it out for several nights. The third night he brought his .45 along and fired three shots at the interpreter. One of them hit its target. The next day he paraded his nude wife through the town to the jail.

26 July

This afternoon Dr. Ting asked us to assist him on a herniorrhaphy. The patient was given spinal anesthesia by Ong (Mr.) Song, the Vietnamese nurse. He was taller than any Vietnamese I had seen. He also was about my age. The anesthetic didn't take well and the patient hopped about a bit with the first incision. Song got the ether machine and started that. Soon, Song reported low blood pressure and Ting had an injection given to raise the blood pressure. Song continued to report low blood pressure and the patient was given two more injections and was about to be given the third when I asked to check the blood pressure myself. Because of the medicine that had been given, it was very high. Likely it was not low in the first place. We watched the patient for a while. There was nothing available to lower the pressure quickly, but soon the pressure began to come down nicely. Unexpectedly, before I knew what had happened, a nurse was directed by Ting to give the man another injection. The medicine was nikethamide, a respiratory stimulant. I could not understand why they gave him this. I advised no further medication be given. The patient did well. Fortunately, none of the Vietnamese personnel seemed insulted by the advice I had given (or so I thought at the time).

Higgins and McCurley chasing cattle.

27 July

Today we got our first look at the surgical ward. We debrided a patient with a ten-day-old, very deep shrapnel wound to the thigh. We were unable to remove the fragment, but it would heal OK as long as infection was kept out through the debridement. A five-year-old girl with a fractured femure was being treated without traction. We started traction. Another small girl was the lone surviving child of a family who had been caught by mortar fire. She had a penetrating wound (three days old) at the right elbow and we debrided this injury. Another child, from whom Dr. Ting had removed an appendix and had given one week of IV penicillin and streptomycin without changing the intercath, had cellulitis of the leg from the intercath. We removed the intercath and started treatment of the cellulitis. There is another man who has an infected amputation of the forearm and we will likely have to amputate this at a higher

site. Thus, there is much basic treatment that we must institute here. Some of the complications could have been avoided by simple measures.

As I look up on the wall of the USAID house [34-h] where I am writing this, I can see six geckos which run about the walls catching insects, particularly mosquitoes. Every now and then they emit a chirping sound.

In the past few days we found a little time to visit the Moc Hoa market [36-a, b, c, d].

28 July

The Special Forces had an operation today. There were dozens of helicopters and 400 Vietnamese troops were loaded into them in groups and carried to the operation area. No contact with the enemy was made but three CIDG (Civilian Irregular Defense Group) troops were injured by mine blasts. They flew them back to our hospital. We were kept busy all day debriding the wounds and removing the shell fragments. All of them were leg wounds. We finished work at 7 p.m. and then attended a going-away party for Major Y., the Special Forces commander. The party was given at the province chief's home. The province chief is a young Vietnamese colonel about 30 years old.

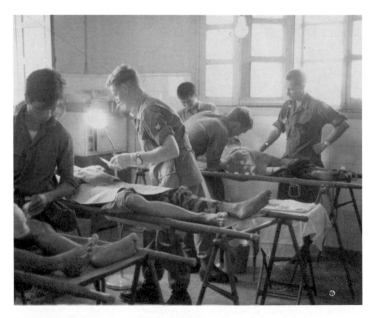

Debriding wounds in surgical building minor surgery room. From left: VN assistant, Boyle, Nguyen, Jackson, myself.

CIDG

The CIDG were Vietnamese troops who had been organized by the Special Forces. There was a Vietnamese Special Forces chain of command in parallel with the U.S. Special Forces and they were in charge of the CIDG. The U.S. Special Forces colonel had a counterpart VN Special Forces colonel. There were majors, captains, lieutenants and sergeants, all counterparts to U.S. personnel. The CIDG were the foot soldiers, the troops for the battle. The U.S. counterparts, though not usually the colonel, went on operations alongside these troops. Many of the local CIDG were *Hoa Hao* (pronounced 'Wah How'). This is a type of Buddhist sect prevalent in a nearby province. The Hoa Hao were no friends of the Communists. Apparently they had been influenced by the French and their religion had intertwinings with the philosophies of Victor Hugo, a French literary champion of liberty, democracy and the common man. Hugo also had a strong faith in God and belief in immortality and the soul. There are others in the CIDG who are not Hoa Hao. And there are some in the CIDG who are VC infiltrators. The infiltrators were felt to be responsible for tipping off the VC in the countryside about impending operations. They were also undoubtedly engaged in activities to discredit the CIDG. For example, wearing the CIDG uniform, they might shoot or steal livestock on operations, thus discrediting the CIDG in the eyes of the local populace. There were rumors of CIDG demanding protection money from some of the local shopkeepers. The VC infiltrators were an enemy in the midst of what were supposed to be friendly troops. During battle the VN and U.S. Special Forces could be at risk, if conditions were right, of being shot from within their own ranks.

29 July

CHOPPERS ON AIRSTRIP

Today was very busy. A much larger operation than Saturday began. The helicopters came from their base somewhere else in the Delta. Early in the morning they came to the airfield which was just across the road from the hospital, giving us a ring-side seat from which to watch. They would at first hover just off the ground, some slowly progressing in one direction and others in the opposite. They seemed like giant prehistoric dragonflies, undecid-ed where to settle down. Finally, they set down, all lined up in a row. The airfield was dirt, perhaps one-half mile in length and the same in width. On the southwest corner was an A-Camp with CIDG. The choppers would batch into smaller groups with their engines and rotors at idle speed. A bunch of CIDG would load in. The choppers would rev up, kick up the dirt, take a short horizontal run and lift off. Meanwhile, the others were idling and loading and in short order the next group would be off. After a few more sorties, they would be all away. The whole procedure would take about half an hour. The sound and sight of this was rather intriguing. First, there was the slow thup, thup of the idling engines and the simultaneous slow whishing of the rotor blades which kept up all during the loading. Then there was the sudden excitement of the sound of the half-dozen choppers accelerating their engines and rotors, churning up the dust. The whine of the engines and the chuf, chuf of the whirling blades then increased in pitch and intensity and rapidly heightened to a final whizzing takeoff. This all seemed a formidable occurrence. In the distance you could still hear the first group, hardly perceptible, but still distinguishable from the last to take off. All this gradually faded out. Out to whatever unique adventure awaited. An adventure of bullets, mines and wounds.

Later in the day the choppers returned, though not all at once. There had been casualties. Some had shrapnel wounds in the extremities and one had a grenade fragment in the abdomen. Dr. Ting is a pretty decent surgeon and he, Jerry and I opened the abdomen. With luck, we found and removed the fragment and closed two small holes in the small bowel. After this case we had the remaining debridements and a shoulder debridement to perform. There had been no instrument packs presterilized and we had to wait between operations for the instruments to be sterilized. We finished at 2 a.m.

30 July

Jerry received a message that his father had died. Arrangements were made to fly him back to the States. This leaves me as the only physician on what was to have been a three-M.D. team.

This morning we also received five or six civilian casualties. One woman was hemorrhaging from the

Now I wish to tell about how I got here. I had been ill Thursday and Friday with diarrhea and some fever and was unable to go to work in the afternoon. Friday evening I had a temperature of 103 degrees two hours after taking two aspirin, and I decided then to go to Saigon to the Third Field Hospital. I got a lift on a Beaver, a small four-seat aircraft. It rained like mad when I arrived and I was thoroughly soaked before I got to the Third Field. They weren't very hospitable and for a while I thought I might not be admitted, which would have put me in quite a predicament because I had nowhere else to go, late at night, in the rain. I was put on the same ward with two other fellows I had sent in a few days before, one with florid jaundice from infectious hepatitis and the other with blood in his urine, the cause being unknown. I stayed there until Monday.

Before leaving I visited the 17th Field Hospital in Saigon and talked with a Mr. Grey, the physical therapist, concerning a partially paralyzed Vietnamese patient in Moc Hoa. The chief of the 17th is a Dr. Withers, whom I know well, for he had been chief of clinical services back at Fort Eustis, Virginia. We worked things out so that the patient could be admitted and treated at the 17th Field Hospital. Then I went back to Tan Son Nhut to try and get a plane back. I had to wait four hours and was able to catch a plane to Can Tho from where it would be easier to get back to Moc Hoa.

Now, to back up to the previous week. There has been some ill feeling lately between my MILPHAP men and the Special Forces here. The relationship between us has never been well defined by anyone, though we are a detachment to their camp. Some of our men are pulling CQ duty, which means that they stay up all night answering calls and are unavailable to work the next day. The sharing of this duty is understandable, but several of my men are key personnel in our functioning at the hospital. Major Conn is reasonable and when I told him that I could not function without one particular man, he was taken off duty.

The sergeant major's attitude toward us had turned confrontational and he had been aggravating the men with minor chores. Then, some days ago, he informed us that half of us would have to move to the A-Team at the airport. The next day I was not feeling well and I asked Sergeant Brown to attend the 6 p.m. briefing, and told him to tell them which of us had agreed to move. After the meeting, Brown told me that the sergeant major said that he would decide who it would be that would go. This, I thought, was a usurping of our command structure. It got me rather teed off and I gave Art Elmore (province USAID ad-

visor) a note and asked him to radio Can Tho, asking Dr. Douglass (MILPHAP coordinator) to define the relationship between Special Forces and our team. Now I knew Art would discuss this with Major Conn, and shortly Art returned to my room to ask what was up. So I related that we were rather unhappy, not about having to move half of us, but about the manner in which we were told to move and its interference in our command structure. Lieutenant Rylant was in Can Tho at the time obtaining supplies and was one of those who would have to move. Bill was hopping mad when he got back and found out about this. Today I personally spoke with Douglass, and we need not pull CQ duty from a command standpoint though he thought it best for us to try and get along in this regard. After the next 6 p.m. meeting, I talked the whole thing over with Major Conn and we sparred a bit over the CQ question which I used as a bargaining chip. As everything worked out, we agreed to pull CQ as before, but in return, we would be able to determine which of us was to move. Actually, if our team had wished to find quarters elsewhere, we had always been free to do so. Then we would have had to handle our own guard duty, so that didn't make any difference as far as CQ was concerned. I really didn't know for sure if it would have been safer to be living in the B-Camp or not. Would the VC pick out the B-Camp as a priority target? If we lived elsewhere, would they tend to leave us alone because we were a medical unit, or would they think we were an easier target than the B-Team and set their sights on us? I thought it better to throw our lot in with the B-Team and not leave that option to the VC.

Thursday 1 September

I met George Marachek briefly after dinner tonight. He discussed plans for building a small hospital near his A-Camp at Kien Quan II. Earlier in the day, Captain Hendricks had asked advice from me on rat eradication. George thought that we shouldn't kill the rats. He recently had a meal of rat at a Vietnamese household.

Sergeant Barry, one of the Special Forces sergeants, has been antagonizing and accusing Higgins of various things the past few days, and I told him in no uncertain terms to lay off my men and if any problems come up with them to see Brown,

Rylant, or me first. I hope he spreads it around that I've had enough of the Special Forces personnel telling us what to do.

(All this sounds as though we had a lot of problems with the Special Forces. Actually, problems were few compared to the cooperation and camaraderie. Basically we liked them a lot. We ate meals with them, played volleyball with them for physical exercise, treated their minor and occasional major ills and played cards and drank with them at the club.)

WANDERING SOULS DAY

Soon to be celebrated are several Vietnamese festivals. We received a description of them. Trung Nguyen or Wandering Souls Day: This festival is also called "The day of the Pardon of the Damned Souls." According to Buddhist belief, the soul lives on after death. The soul that does not enter Buddhist Nirvana or is not reincarnated immediately, will need help. Those souls, whose faults are not balanced with good actions, will be punished in one of several hells. Buddhism teaches that a soul can be absolved from punishment by prayers said by the living on the first or 15th of each month. But, Wandering Souls Day is the best opportunity to secure general amnesty.

On this day the gates of hell are opened at sunset and the "damned" souls fly out naked and hungry. Those who have relatives return to their homes and find plenty of food on their family altars. Those with no one to pray or perform ceremonies for them are dependent on charity. They are feared because, cold and hungry, they may harm the living. To prevent this, prayers and offerings are made. A special meal is prepared in private homes at nightfall. Tables, containing all kinds of food, fruits and cakes, are set up in front of homes. Votive papers and coins of small denominations (which will later be given to children) are also placed on the tables. Incense is burned and all members of the household join the prayer, inviting the souls to the feast. Rice and salt are scattered as offerings and the votive papers are burned.

Votive papers simulate giving the real thing. Money, horses, clothing, or anything the departed soul might need, are symbolized on these papers. Burning them is traditional in many Vietnamese ceremonies but is especially important in this one. Its origin is unknown, but it is said to have been introduced by a Chinese Mandarin, Vuang Du, of the Han Dynasty. At that time in China, the people were compelled to observe a blind loyalty toward a despotic ruler. They were buried with him so as to serve him in the other world. This practice disappeared when Vuang Du substituted the burning of votive papers for the living sacrifices.

Ceremonies also take place in large pagodas. Free vegetarian meals are offered to everybody. The poor come to the pagoda with their families in the belief that food from Buddha brings good luck. In the afternoon, tables are heaped with all kinds of candy, cakes and fruits brought by the faithful or purchased by the pagoda. A large quantity of votive papers is mixed with the delicacies. By late evening, the pagoda is filled with an immense crowd. In the midst of burning incense and lighted candles, prayers are said, inviting the spirits to the feast and asking for clemency for the souls. Those souls not granted amnesty must return to their torments.

Butcher shops are especially careful to observe this holiday. According to Buddhist teachings, human beings are subject to nine paths of reincarnation. That is, after death, a man can become an animal and, inversely, an animal can become a man. Thus, a butcher who kills a pig or cow might unknowingly kill his father or his mother in their animal reincarnations and for these crimes, he would be doomed to damnation. In order to avoid this, he must strictly observe the Vu Lan service on Wandering Souls Day — kill no beasts whatsoever, large or small, and eat no meat.

Tuesday 6 September

The election is to be held in a few days — on the 11th. The town here has been placed off-limits and the guard at the compound has been doubled due to increased and anticipated VC activity.

They ran an operation today up in the finger region. Captain Bridgewater and his Vietnamese Special Forces troops were involved. For some time it had been known that the VC had prepared positions adjacent to the Cambodian border in this region. Yesterday a plane flying over the area received heavy fire from these positions. Bridgewater's men advanced northward up the finger toward the positions and began to receive light fire from the southwest, across the border. On approaching the positions they received some fire from the positions themselves and heavier fire from the southwest. Then they began to

Helicopter bringing casualties. Barton and Kelly carrying stretcher.

also receive heavy fire from the northeast from across the border and decided to withdraw. One of his men was hit in the neck and was evacuated to us. The man was very fortunate — had the bullet passed one inch to the left, it would have severed his spinal cord or, one inch the other way, and it would have severed his carotid artery. Several others received minor wounds. One round went through a radio a VN trooper was carrying on his back. The bullet protruded half-way through the back of the radio, not harming the man. A mortar was not functioning properly and because of this and the heavy fire, the troops, of necessity, had to withdraw from the area.

LETTER HOME

I have been writing letters to various places back home and thought I would repeat their contents here.

I have now been in Vietnam nearly two months at Moc Hoa [36-e, f, g], a village of 7,000 located in the Mekong Delta, Plain of Reeds, 50 miles west of Saigon and five miles from the Cambodian border. Our team has 14 medical personnel, three of whom were to be physicians. Due to illness, only two physi-

cians arrived, and because of the death of the father of the other, I have been quite alone here for the past month. This team is one of 15 or so MILPHAP teams now in the country. We are designed to implement the care of patients in a hospital located in a provincial capital. Some of our enlisted men are conscientious objectors. Most of the teams at present are in the Delta. We have a pharmacist, lab technician, X-ray technician, operating room technician and other military men with varying skills [53-b].

The men are housed at the Special Forces compound. Rylant and I are staying at the USAID house which is near the river and one-half mile down the road from the compound. Each morning we drive our jeep down to the compound for breakfast. Then we all head down in the jeeps to the hospital which is another half-mile farther down the road.

Our hospital consists of five buildings with a capacity of 100 beds [35-a, b, c, e, f]. The main building has a small office, a 50-bed medical ward and a 15-bed tuberculosis ward. There is a separate surgical ward building with 25 beds and a maternity building with 15 beds. Midwives handle all the routine deliveries. We have another building consisting of operating room, minor surgery room and recovery room. The newest of the buildings is a combination outpatient/office area, a laboratory area [53-h] and a room for X-ray. There was much more in the way of physical facilities here than we had anticipated. The upkeep of the place is something different again. The roof leaks badly in the newest building. The screens all have holes, flies abound, and the people persist in throwing garbage on the hospital grounds.

Prior to our arrival, the hospital was handled by one VN military physician, 34 years old, who is quite intelligent and speaks English fairly well. Currently he has been relieved from hospital duties to campaign for the coming elections. He seems fairly competent as far as certain procedures such as herniorrphaphy, appendectomy and so forth are concerned, but is not very good as a pediatrician, physiologist, or pharmacologist.

Nursing personnel had been in charge of the actual care of most of the patients, especially the medical patients. The first day that I made rounds on the medical ward I was surprised to find nearly every patient on intramuscular injections of camphor and nikethamide. They admitted that unless the patient received an injection (''chit'' as they called it), he would not be impressed with the treatment rendered and would be likely to leave. Thus, patients having things from infectious hepatitis to ascariasis were all receiving camphor and nikethamide. Apparently this is a leftover from an old French method of treatment.

Let me tell you about the patients that are now on the wards. Surgical ward: bed 1 — herniorrphaphy patient done yesterday; bed 2 — an appendectomy, two weeks old, with some drainage from the incision site which is clearing; bed 3 — a man with a bullet wound through the shoulder, debrided four days ago; bed 4 — a four-year-old girl, whom we have in traction, with a fracture of the mid-shaft of the femur. There is one centimeter of overriding and good alignment and according to Dr. Blount's book, should heal without complication. (Dr. Blount is a famous orthopedist whom I had as a lecturer in medical school in Milwaukee.) Bed 5 — a man with right lower quadrant abdominal pain (we discovered a large infestation with ascaris after having done exploratory surgery for possible appendicitis); beds 6 and 7 — Vietnamese soldiers with bullet wounds of the leg which we debrided a few days ago; bed 8 — an old woman with post concussion headaches; bed 9 — a man whose lateral aspect of the left foot was blown apart by a mine (he has granulated in well and the other day we put a skin graft on the area); bed 10 — an old man with cellulitis of the foot and a scaling mycotic (fungal) infection over the rest of his body; bed 11 — a man recently shot through the cheek while loading his gun; beds 12, 13, 14 and 15 — amputees awaiting shipment to Saigon for prostheses; bed 16 — a woman from whom we removed an ectopic pregnancy with massive bleeding into the abdominal cavity.

Medical ward: One-quarter of the patients have vague abdominal pain, in many of these cases we find ascaris, hookwork and whipworm; one-quarter of the initial ward patients likely had tuberculosis. We confirmed the diagnosis by X-ray and sputum smear on most of these and have transferred them to the tuberculosis ward. We have four patients with infectious hepatitis, one with heart failure and a few with pneumonia. We have four children with pneumonia and two with diarrhea. A few of the patients are malingerers using the hospital for a hotel.

I have been seeing 15 to 20 outpatients each day and have found four or five new cases of tuberculosis each day. The main cause of death in Vietnam is TB. The second is malaria, although there isn't much in the Delta.

Some weeks ago a Dr. James Carraway, a surgeon from one of the other teams, arrived. In the past he had corrected upwards of 100 hairlips and over a five-day period, we corrected eight here, the last two of which I did without his assistance. The number of people in Vietnam with this deformity is large.

10 September

Yesterday the VC ambushed two Vietnamese patrols, one south of A-Camp 416 and the other, north of 415. There were no serious casualties.

I had two disagreements today. The first was with Bill this morning. Yesterday a new chief MSC officer from Saigon arrived to discuss our problems and told Bill that he need not be so careful with things. Our property upon our departure would be given to the Vietnamese. He also told Bill that he need not wait and check for approval before using the accessory fund for the hospital. So this morning I told Bill to hire some of the Chieu Hoi (former VC) laborers to add fill to the hospital grounds. He promptly told me he would have to write first and check to see if it would be OK. I told him to forget about writing and do it. He told me he was in charge of the money, and I told him I was the commander of the unit and to go do it. He said he wouldn't be responsible and I retorted that I would. This sounds like we had arguments all the time but that wasn't true. We usually get along fine and he does his job very well.

The second problem was with McCurley who closed the pharmacy without checking with me while I still had five outpatients to see. I had him return from lunch to open it up.

Sunday 11 September

Most of the morning was spent removing grenade fragments from several Vietnamese and casting a broken arm. We were headed for the A-Camp at the airport where there were two Mohawks and their pilots [34-g]. The planes are in and out of Moc Hoa several times each day. The squadron of 17 Mohawks is located at Vung Tau and covers the border areas of Second, Third and Fourth Corps. These are small, fighter-bomber type, two-propeller aircraft originally designed in 1959 for the Navy and are now used by the Army. They fire rockets from three pods on each wing.

My interpreter, Nguyen Houie, is a Buddhist. I thought I would like to learn something about Buddhism and at dinner tonight I asked him some things. The Buddhist strives continuously to be a more perfect and noble man. In this way, he will — in future lives or the hereafter — receive a better position. They believe in reincarnation; thus, a man in future lives may return as an object, animal, or another man. The Buddhist strives to do good and follows ideals similar to the Commandments. They should not kill, steal, or commit adultery. The purists of the Buddhists are vegetarians, for they believe they should kill no living thing.

Suddenly machine-gun fire erupted near the downtown area, six blocks away. There were explosions and incoming mortar rounds. An alert was called and Dr. Taylor (our civilian volunteer temporary surgeon) and I scrambled out of the room. I grabbed my .38 revolver and put it in my right pocket, grabbed 50 of the .38 shells and put them in the left, put on

Jackson and Kelly painting the lab.

my helmet, grabbed my carbine and two 30-shot clips and ran to the medical shack where I am stationed for alerts. There was no further shooting and after 15 minutes the all-clear sounded. There was some uncertainty as to what had occurred, but it likely was an exchange of fire between friendly forces and then close mortar rounds put in by the Vietnamese troops. Tonight, by the way, is election night.

15 September

Dr. Ting placed fifth of the candidates. The day after the election, his driver informed me that he was so sad that he went to Saigon for a week to recuperate. More likely just another excuse to take a vacation.

Today in the office while examining a patient, I stepped lightly on something hard under the rug. I lifted the corner of the rug and found a large lizard. The female patient I was examining jumped when she saw it.

Somebody at the compound caught an eight-foot python out somewhere and the Special Forces people were taking pictures of it and trying to feed it some ducks. Though only captured yesterday, the snake was easily handled and apparently not about to bite so I held it and had one of the fellows take my picture [53-e].

We got word today that Jerry Farber, the other M.D. who came over with me, has been reassigned to the States for compassionate reasons. That leaves me as the only one of the original three M.D.'s. I've been overly busy at the hospital and am going to push for some replacements.

It was late afternoon and Dr. Taylor and I were in the surgical building involved in some smaller procedure. One of the midwives came and told us that a woman who had been in labor for some time was "getting very tired." So I went with her to see the patient. I came back and told Taylor that the head was up high yet and that we should decide if we could

with bags. It was hard, physical, muddy, satisfying work. The outer wall of the compound was sandbagged to a height of four feet and the water was starting to come up the outside of the wall.

ESCAPE

Mr. Houie got away today. He showed up at the hospital and asked if he could leave. I told him, "No," and that he should send a telegram to Saigon, which he did. At noon he said he must leave and that he didn't think he would receive a reply to the telegram. I said he could leave, but without permission, which meant it would cost him his job, though if he should come back I probably would hire him again. A week ago I had bawled out the men at the airport for not getting Houie on a plane to Can Tho to pick up his check. Now Houie simply showed up at the airport, which can handle only helicopters, and he told the men that I had said he must be taken to Saigon — which I did not say — and they got him on a helicopter. That will likely be the last we'll see of Houie.

Houie had impressed me as being a namby-pamby (sissy). I thought the rest of us were toughing it out here and it wouldn't hurt him to get a little tougher also. He had complained about water being in the lower floor of where he was sleeping, so I arranged for him to sleep in the X-ray building which was still dry. The following morning he discovered that he had shared the room with a small snake. He was quite shaken by this and decided to return to where he had been staying before.

Sunday 25 September

THE FLOOD [54-d, e]

The flood is upon us. I feel a bit like Noah. The water is six inches up on the sandbags around our camp and we're keeping out the seepage with pumps. Most of the houses in town are under water and the market is just starting to go under. An immunization team came in today from Me Tho and we have started to give cholera and typhoid vaccinations. Our men were in the market all afternoon and inoculated about 250 people, most of them children. The adults are reluctant to be inoculated. Dr. Ting had a four-man team going door to door giving immunizations so we've got a good start. There is three feet of water on the hospital grounds, but the wards are not yet flooded. I just stopped to spray my room. There are many ants which are seeking high ground. Tomorrow I'm going to chlorinate the city water supply. The airfield is now four feet under water.

One of the A-Camps to the north has three to four feet of water in the camp. There are only two small dry areas in the province to the northwest of us and many people are crowded into these areas. We have many refugees on the higher ground in Moc Hoa. Most of these are from the lower areas of town.

I worked very hard today getting the vaccination business organized and arranged for the chlorination of the city water and the boiling of water at the hospital.

Fifteen rounds went off about a block from here, likely a policeman firing at someone.

Monday 26 September

The waters continue to rise at the same rapid rate. Today the immunization team went down to the market [54-f], but had little luck there. USAID set up a food station. We arranged things such that to get food the people would have to receive immunizations first. This worked.

General Humphries flew in today to look over the situation. I met him at the hospital at 9 a.m. and we discussed what was being done about the medical problems caused by the flood. I described our immunization program and our plans to chlorinate the city water. Shortly after he arrived an explosion occurred in a housing area to the west of the hospital and a large fire started [54-g, h, i]. Then, we received five burn cases. Two children were dead, and a man and a child were severely burned. We began working on these patients. General Humphries left shortly thereafter. We found out later that the people had been cooking on top of a 55-gallon drum that still had fuel in it.

Tomorrow we're setting up five teams to begin immunizations in the district towns. This afternoon I went to the public works center and contacted a Mr. Lien who runs the water plant. They have an eight-month-old plant which is very modern. There is excellent equipment there for chlorinating the water continuously and they know how to use it, but hadn't been because of the bad taste that it gave the water. Tomorrow the water will be chlorinated.

Lieutenant Rylant in sampan taxi.

Thursday 29 September [55-a, b, c, d]

The flood waters are slowing in their rise. We're continuing to inoculate for typhoid and cholera and have now immunized 2,000 city residents and have teams out in the district towns [55-e]. Today we received an assault boat with a 35-horsepower Mercury motor, and this will be a big help in the immunization program. I wonder if Humphries had a hand in helping us get this. I think I've now got the Vietnamese at the water plant properly chlorinating the water. We'll test it tomorrow and see.

MUD CHAIN

In the middle of the night I awoke to a commotion one room down at the compound wall and heard water flowing. Soon we were all shagged out in our bare feet and underwear. Some of the sandbags had given way and water was coming into the compound. By now the water had risen up to almost three feet

on the outside of the sandbags. Quickly we formed a human chain and in the dark of night passed the reserve sandbags, which were my latrine bags, over to the break in the wall. I was in the middle of the chain. The ground was muddy from the constant seepage and the bags came heavy and wet. Some were making a game of it, heaving the bags at the one next in line to see if they could make him fall. Every so often someone lost his balance and fell down into the mud with the bag. Wet mud dripped — from arms and down the abdomen and down the legs. After awhile we had it plugged. We weren't a pretty sight, but we had the satisfaction of having kept the water out.

Friday [55-g]

This morning we were coming into one of the school areas where many refugees are housed and as we were set to dock I spotted some people with a wooden crate containing two large cobras. It was tied to the spot where our boat was headed. We couldn't stop the boat in time and nearly smashed into the cobra crate. The snakes, I was told by my interpreter, were harmless because they were drugged by the people so that they would not bite. Also, their mouths were sewn shut with loops of a thick thread. The people were planning to eat them.

Tonight we were called to come down to the hospital. There we found a dead Vietnamese lieutenant. He had been electrocuted, and there was nothing we could do for him. Undoubtedly the wet conditions had been responsible for this.

Sunday 2 October [55-f]

Several things have occurred. Yesterday, we got the 35-horsepower mercury working and were on our way to the A-Camp when we noted a Caribou cargo plane coming for us. He was going to drop supplies. We were in the drop zone and he was definitely aiming for us. Directly overhead he nosed up and the cargo, all with parachutes attached, fell out of the back of the plane. Shortly the large packages were directly overhead. Jackson didn't think very fast, for instead of opening the throttle wide, he made a circle at low throttle with all of us yelling at him to open it up. When he finally opened it up, the nearest item, about the size of the boat, landed only 30 yards away. We were ready to jump.

Today the starter rope broke and we tried to paddle down to the hospital, but halfway there the wind began moving us back. I thought it was three feet deep and thought I'd jump out and push. Well, it was six feet. I went in over my head and got a good soaking.

Today they brought in two VC. We took a .45 slug out of one man. The other had a bullet in his chest and had a hemo-pneumothorax (blood and air in the lung). We put a chest tube in and fixed him up.

3 October

Some big operations are planned. They're getting in many gunboats (airboats with machine guns mounted on them) and now have 30 to 40 assault boats with motors. The flood is the worst since 1892.

4 October

WESTMORELAND

Today was a most interesting day. General Westmoreland arrived at 9:30 a.m. The 12 or so officers here with the B-Team (including me) shook hands with him on arrival. Dr. Bill Taylor got some good photos. We then proceeded to the colonel's office where the general was given a briefing in turn by each of the officers concerning the situation in the province, particularly in reference to the flood. I had the opportunity to personally give the general a briefing on the medical aspects, informing him of the hospital situation, the immunization program and our efforts to provide potable water to the people. The general was pleased with the military and social efforts that we were putting forth.

My briefing with General Westmoreland went as follows:

Kammholz "Sir, I'm Captain Kammholz, medical officer with the MILPHAP team here. We have been here two months now. There are 12 members in addition to myself and two temporary physicians. Of course we're concerned mainly at present with the flood situation. Particularly, we are concerned with immunization against cholera and typhoid and providing potable water. The city water has been chlorinated and we are encouraging use of only boiled water by the civilian population. We have now immunized 7,000 persons in the province, including 2,500 in Moc Hoa and are pleased with the program at present. We have had only two cases of suspected typhoid and are surprised that we have not had more disease thus far."

Westmoreland "What is the situation at the hospital?"

Kammholz "The wards are under one-half foot of water and we are attempting to pump this out of the main room. We are continuing to function and have surgical and medical capability, but are treating as many as possible on an outpatient basis or are evacuating them to another hospital."

Westmoreland "Is the hospital well equipped? When I was here last year they were just starting with the building program."

Kammholz "The hospital at present is adequately equipped."

Westmoreland "Do you have a Vietnamese physician? Is he ARVIN or civilian, and do you work hand in hand with him?"

Kammholz "Yes, we have a Vietnamese physician. He is ARVIN (Vietnamese Army) and I work quite closely with him."

Westmoreland "How is the sanitation situation in the various A-Camps?"

Kammholz "Sir, I have not personally inspected the sanitation situation at these camps."

Colonel D. "The sanitation at the camps is good. We take care of our own sanitation." (Colonel D. was from a Special Forces headquarters unit to which our B-Team was connected.)

Westmoreland "Thank you, Doctor."

The general then stood and told us, as I had said before, that he was very impressed with how things were going militarily and civic wise in the province [56-a].

4 October continued

In the afternoon Dr. Ting, McCurley and I boarded an Air America helicopter and flew down to Ap Bac [56-b], a town of about 3,000 located to the southwest of Moc Hoa. A Captain Strand, with his Med-Cap team from My Tho, was supposed to be giving immunizations in that area. He had done nothing and had gone, we discovered. We were left off one-quarter mile from town on the only high ground and had to wade in chest high water to the town. Ting fell and dunked McCurley's $100 camera and my .38 revolver. We arrived at a long, high bridge on which were jammed many vehicles. We met a U.S. lieutenant there who took us to meet the other three U.S. personnel in Ap Bac at their small compound.

We had coffee and discussed the water situation at the compound. They had a good water system with filtration and chlorination and were well set in that area. We then went over to the district chief's office. There were two ''floors,'' one consisting of planks elevated by barrels on both ends of the office. At one end were the office workers and at the other the chief's desk and a tea table. We discussed informing the people to drink only boiled water or tea and gave the chief 50 pamphlets in Vietnamese to pass among the people. He said he would have more run off on his duplicating machine. We then discussed immunizations. Dr. Ting planned to bring an immunization team in tomorrow to stay for several days and also to immunize persons in several surrounding towns. So, the afternoon was likely well spent. After a while, the chopper returned and took us back to Moc Hoa.

Thursday 6 October

Last night several of us went to the USAID house to play bridge with Terry Walsh, Bob Bridgen (a temporary M.D. here) and Max (a USAID worker). Because of the flood we weren't able to drive and walking would get us considerably wet. So, over the compound sandbags just outside the gate, we got into a rowboat that had an outboard on it. We started it up and motored down the street through the dimly moonlit night. I was sitting on the front edge of the boat with my back facing to the front and my head turned slightly forward. Just past the province chief's house I saw the white flash of an underwater object go by. The boat hit the concrete block and jolted abruptly to a stop. Without a chance to react or grab onto anything I was flipped backward, over the bow, headfirst into the water and down under into an instantaneous, drenching disorientation. I floundered about, then slowly struggled to my feet and came up soaked and bewildered, but laughing. I felt lucky — lucky that I wasn't hurt and thankful that it wasn't a VC ambush.

Today Dr. Ting, Dr. Bridgen, Jackson and I took an Air America helicopter into Tuyen Nhon. Just after lifting off the ground at Moc Hoa we noted two skyraiders. These are piloted by Vietnamese. They followed us for a while and flew around in wide circles. Then they both came at us directly from our rear and one passed over the top and the other under the bottom of us. Then they dipped close to the ground as if to attack a ground target. This all was quite entertaining, but we wondered if they might have had a fleeting thought about shooting us down.

We arrived at A-Camp 415 which is five kilometers from Tuyen Nhon. There I talked over the camp immunization status with the medic — a full-blooded American Indian. After lunch we took an assault boat with sampan motor into Tuyen Nhon. Food was being distributed in town and Dr. Ting spoke with the civic action worker there to have him announce over his loudspeaker that tomorrow, in order to get food, they would have to be immunized. Dr. Ting had a team in this area last week. This team worked hard and was able to immunize 1,000 of the 4,000 total population of the district. We gave immunization materials to the local medic and should be able to immunize still more in this way.

On getting back to the A-Camp we found that close to the Cambodian border they had captured two VC today. Many documents were captured, including certificates of achievement for VC, medical pamphlets, a Chinese karate book, a commander's evaluation of his men, VC newspapers and many other papers and pamphlets. Dr. Ting translated a portion of the commander's report. This certain VC was reluctant to fight and wished to be with a noncombatant radio team. The commander was going to bring him to a tribunal. Another VC was described as a good VC. He had thrown five grenades in the past month and so forth.

Dr. Taylor, Ting, Jackson and I took an Air America helicopter to Long Kot today [56-c, d, e, f]. This is an area to the northwest and is hardest hit by the flood. We met the district chief and discussed the flood situation over tea. Long Kot is only 500 meters from Cambodia. We asked if it would be possible to take a few photos a few yards inside of Cambodia. Dr. Ting thought it would be perfectly safe, but I later learned that the district chief had some concern, not for safety, but that he would be responsible if some incident should occur. Ting, Taylor, Jackson, a boat driver and I then headed for the border in an assault boat with an Evinrude engine. The water was very shallow and the engine kept hitting bottom. At the border area were a number of huts and one large tree which was said to be just over the border. Here we took some photos.

About 50 yards away, Ting noticed a Cambodian town chief, and called to him that he should come and get his picture taken. He called back and declined our offer and stated that he was afraid of us (Jackson and I were in military uniform). He was afraid of the possibility that we might capture him and take him into Vietnam. Upon learning this from Ting I thought for a moment what I could reply. It was completely ridiculous from our standpoint that we should try to capture him, but I understood his caution. I told Ting to tell him this and then we waved good-by to him and left immediately for the boat. I also had mentioned my uneasiness to Ting several times during this excursion to the border, but Ting kept stating to me that I worried unnecessarily. So today I set foot in Cambodia. I had wished to be friendly to this Cambodian and shake his hand and talk with him, but there was a double border. The other was the border of uncertainty and mistrust that prevented our meeting. It was an absurd border for there was no truth to the fear behind it. How often are there borders like this?

Higgins and Nelson returned from a three-day supply trip to Saigon today. They stayed at the Saigon Hotel and ate every night at a French restaurant called La Cave.

Art Elmore, the USAID representative, arrived drunk at the compound. He tipped his boat over at the gate and cut his hand on barbed wire and stormed into the club calling the Special Forces "damned green beanies." One of the sergeants slugged him and knocked him down. The results of this should be interesting.

I forgot to mention that there are 8,000 people in Tuyen Binh (the district that I visited today). Long Kot usually has 1,500 people. With the floods there are now 3,500. Also in the district, according to some charts in the district chief's office, are 26 cows, 900 water buffalo, 1,300 pigs and 10,000 chickens. The town is made up of refugees from North Vietnam who emigrated there in 1956.

Saturday 15 October

Three days ago we were called to go to the airport helipad to await arrival of a Medivac helicopter which was going to refuel on the way to Saigon. A Sergeant Menophie had been shot in an operation at 416. We hurried to the pad in our boat. Soon the helicopter arrived. The sergeant had been shot in the back of the head and things looked bad. We started an IV and two of us accompanied him into Saigon in the helicopter. Yesterday I learned he had died. He was the first American killed in this area since my arrival.

Sunday

Last Thursday Mr. Song held a party in Saigon at his 78-year-old mother's villa for Co Chan, his daughter, who is to be married in January. Art Elmore, Max (his assistant), Mrs. Gallager (our temporary

I brought this old man back in a helicopter from Long
Kot. He had been staying at the small dispensary there
and had been gradually weakening. I had gone there
on some other business, but the Vietnamese in charge
of the clinic asked if I would take him back to Moc
Hoa to see if we could help him. He rode back beside
me in the helicopter. He was feeble, and needed my
assistance in walking from the landing area to the hospital.

nurse-anesthetist) and I attended. We arrived a bit late and the food was somewhat cold, but nevertheless it was an interesting evening. The villa is on the outskirts of Saigon, and I was somewhat concerned about my safety. Fifteen minutes before the 11 p.m. curfew Mr. Song helped us hail a taxi to take us back to the USAID guest house in Saigon.

After returning, Art got to talking to Kay Gallager and me about some of his recent problems. Several nights prior to the party Art was in the club at about 5 p.m. and got into an exchange of insults with one of the Special Forces' officers. The officer called him a quitter from the Army, among other things. Art had formerly been in Special Forces and, for reasons unknown to me, gave this up to work for USAID. Art said that then he left and over the next hour drank half of a Johnny Walker's. He then returned to the compound and on his way in cut his hand on the barbed wire at the gate. He stormed into the club and began to vociferously berate the Special Forces, aiming it at a sergeant friend of his. After five minutes of this, the sergeant could stand no more and slugged Art in the mouth, knocking him to the floor. Art told me that he recognized that the incident was mostly his fault and that he was worried about his job as a province representative if this should get out.

Previously Art had worked in Laos, I believe with the Special Forces. Then he joined USAID and was assigned as a refugee officer in one of the northern provinces, but this job was nearly nonexistent at that province because of certain circumstances. Then he was briefly transferred to work with the Montagnards and then to working as a temporary province representative. He was in an area where a certain general had jurisdiction, and they did not get along well. One night he and several others were folk-singing and were apprehended for disorderly conduct by some of the general's MP's. He told them they had no authority to apprehend him for this but was detained and without being given opportunity to explain to USAID, was transferred to work here as province representative. This place is considered by some USAID province representatives to be the Siberia of Vietnam. This explains Art's concern for his job after the latest incidents.

This afternoon, Song, Nguyen (our Vietnamese lab technician), Taylor, several of the team and I took the boat out on the canal and went swimming. We found out later that Nguyen wasn't much of a swimmer. He jumped in off the boat and missed the inner tube and had to be rescued. I thought about maybe getting some water skis rigged up. (The boats we had would have worked well for this. From several different perspectives I could visualize the bizarreness of the situation. This never came about — mainly because we had no skis.)

Monday 17 October

Last night we received seven patients who had been injured by a mine. The man who picked it up had both hands blown off and his face was completely macerated. He lost his nose and both eyes.

They had a big operation yesterday down in "The Pocket." This is an area which has been under VC control for more than ten years. They captured 125 weapons and killed 25 VC with no friendly casualties. Assault boats with 35- and 40-horsepower motors were used in the operation.

18 October

General Humphries and the new Vietnamese minister of health, with his aides, and Dr. Douglass, visited us today. Douglass is the civilian M.D. coordinator of the MILPHAP teams. We again discussed the flood situation and then took a motorboat to Bien Hiep to survey the damage caused by the flood to the medical facilities there. Bien Hiep is several miles up the river near Cambodia. The clinic there had been blown up by the VC a half year ago so the damage there had already been done. We're going to rebuild that place after the flood.

It was a grey overcast day. We went back down the river full throttle, standing up in the open launch. On the way I thought the VC could make quite a haul if they were ready for us — General Humphries, the entire Ministry of Health, Ting and me. After we got back we took a helicopter to Long Kot and had a conference with the district chief there. Then we returned to Moc Hoa and had lunch with the province chief.

Friday

Yesterday they continued to have success on operations. More than 2,000 grenades and 35 VC were captured.

Last night Long Kot was attacked by an estimated 80 VC. Small arms and 16 mortar rounds hit the district headquarters and camp. Six VN soldiers were killed and today we received four wounded civilians. This is the place I had visited with General Humphries and the others three days ago.

Wednesday 26 October

Today A-413 had an operation and exchanged fire with the VC across the Cambodian border. Five VN troops were killed and two American Special Forces advisors wounded. Fourteen VC were known killed. Our B-Team (B-41) with its four A-detachments has the best VC/friendly troop kill ratio in all Vietnam.

Today we received 14 airboats. When the water goes down slightly, the conditions will be just right for their use.

Monday, the commander at A-415 (Tuyen Nhon) reported that there was a possible epidemic of a serious diarrheal illness at their location. Three of my team, Nguyen and I flew down to investigate [56-g]. One VN soldier at the A-Camp had clinical typhoid. One child had died the day before and several other people had gone to the hospital at the neighboring province. I was told that 20 persons were seriously ill near a Catholic church down the river [56-h]. The next morning we visited the church and Father Louis. He called in eight of the sick persons. These were mostly children who had only mild diarrhea, certainly not typhoid. Father Louis had had some medical training and had purchased some medicine with which he had treated people. I left him a small supply of medication.

We spent the next day and a half waiting for a chopper to get back to Moc Hoa. The first night at A-415 I slept in a room with rats running all night on the false ceiling and with several occasionally chewing on things in the room. One of them scuttled across the top and then down the side of the mosquito netting under which I was sleeping. The next night I was able to sleep in Corporal Vey's room while he was on guard duty. Shortly after getting in bed I heard a loud rustling under the bed. I thought that this must be a large rat. I shined my flashlight under the bed and found three puppies which Vey had been raising for the past month. About five minutes later one of them started tugging on the mosquito net. Be-

ing tired, I shoved him away and he went to the room across the hall and started barking at a bug on the floor.

I returned to Moc Hoa at noon. This afternoon, Nelson and Brown were in front of the surgical suite working on the boat motor when a rifle round splashed in the water about a yard from Nelson. I was standing at the door about ten yards away. Nelson thought it came from the A&L Company 100 yards to the east of the hospital. Likely a VN trooper was out to have some fun by scaring them. Mr. Song went to investigate and we notified the B-Team and local police.

29 October

Yesterday a Chieu Hoi (VC returnee) was caught making a map of the B-Team compound here. Today they apprehended three others who were implicated by the one caught yesterday. One of these had been working in the compound. They were interrogated and it was found that the information had been requested by a new VC commander to the south of here. The former commander had been killed some weeks ago.

Monday 31 October

I was talking with Dr. Ting at the club yesterday morning and I mentioned having seen Father Louis in Tuyen Nhon. Dr. Ting mentioned that Father Louis had a pretty maid and that he wished to leave the priesthood and get married. He also mentioned that a certain sergeant at A-415 who has a wife in the States was spending his third tour here and that he had volunteered for the third tour because of a Vietnamese girl he knew in Saigon.

This morning, as per the past few mornings, I heard frequent rumblings in the distance. I'm told that this is bombing going on 60 miles away to the north. When the B-52's bombed just north of here six months ago there was no shock wave in Moc Hoa. The bombs burrowed quite deeply into the mud before exploding and then the blast shot nearly straight up through the entrance channel having little effect on even huts as much as 30 yards away.

BORDER INCIDENT

Art Elmore returned from Saigon yesterday and brought Inka, a German dancer, along. While flying in the helicopter on the way here she decided to change into tiger fatigues. Now, if Inka were a real good looker, this might be serious stuff, but Inka was no bombshell; in fact, she was even a bit unattractive and indeed, more than sufficiently fat. Anyway, the pilots were quite amused. This was undoubtedly the first time their helicopter had been used as a dressing room by a strip-tease dancer. While this distraction was going on, the helicopter drifted to the north and meandered over about 20 miles of Cambodian territory. At this time, border incidents were considered serious matters. I could see the headlines back in the States, ''Cambodia protests provocative intrusion by U.S. helicopter.'' Art brought her to the camp this evening where she put her act on in the club. Everyone applauded and cheered. She went back to USAID where nobody paid her any attention and Art had her flown back to Saigon the next day. I think Art may have brought her here to help patch up things between him and the Special Forces after their recent disagreements. On the other hand, maybe not, for the whole episode would best be described as a comic interlude.

Monday 31 October continued

Concerning the floods again — the Tonle Sap is a lake 80 by 20 miles in central Cambodia. Flood waters from the Mekong flow to the junction of a river flowing from the Tonle Sap toward Vietnam. These flood waters back up the river going back to the Tonle Sap which normally runs toward Vietnam. The lake grows to twice its normal size. At this point the lake can accommodate no more flood water and the Mekong flood waters proceed into Vietnam.

Tuesday 1 November

There are three battalions of VC to the north of us in Cambodia, not more than 20 miles away. Captain Smith believes the most logical target for that size unit would be Moc Hoa.

Wednesday 2 November

THE TAX COLLECTOR

I have just finished a talk with Captain Marachek of A-416 to the south of here. He asked to go to the hospital to see a Vietnamese patient whom his men had shot by accident several days ago. Dr. Taylor was still here then (he left two days ago). The bullet had pierced the colon and bladder and an extensive operation had been necessary to repair these injuries. While at the hospital Captain Marachek mentioned that I must have another patient of his — a 12-year-old VC boy — who had been wounded in the shoulder. Dr. Bridgen (my temporary helper during the flood) had taken care of him. Several days ago Bridgen had told me about how the boy glared at him while he was treating the injury.

About a week ago Captain Marachek was out on a motorboat operation in ''The Pocket'' area south of A-416 near the province border. Prior to the flood, Vietnamese troops were unable to enter this area. It was all VC and had been so for many years. Captain Marachek spotted two objects under the water. A man and this boy were hiding beneath the water by breathing through reeds. Captain Marachek pulled the boat over and pulled up on the reeds and out of the water they came. The man had a brand new U.S. shotgun in his possession. A fight ensued, and the man was killed and the boy wounded in the shoulder.

This man was the chief VC tax collector for the district and had many underling tax collectors working for him. These collectors take only rice and other food from the VC sympathizers. From South Vietnamese sympathizers traveling with cargo by boat up the canals they collect money — $20 at a time. They threaten to kill them and take away their cargo if they do not pay.

The boy turned out to be the son of the collector. Small wonder he glared at us.

Wednesday 10 November

I have spent the past five days out of town. I had some matters to discuss with Douglass in Can Tho. Dr. Ting had left for Saigon several days earlier and invited me to visit him, so after spending Saturday and Sunday in Can Tho, Williams and I flew to Saigon to see Ting. When members of our team make such excursions, we travel with at least one other of the team for safety reasons. Ting was staying at his mother's home — an apartment in downtown Saigon. It was comparable to a good apartment in the U.S. The floor had decorative tile and he had a good record-player with U.S. records. After some time there we left and went back to stay at USAID.

The next morning Ting and I went to Hong Bong tuberculosis hospital. This was a low, light tan building in a cleaner and less bustling section of the city than the downtown area where Ting's apartment had been. There we met the National Director of TB control in his pleasant office surroundings with windows looking out upon palm foliage. This Vietnamese M.D. had spent 20 years in France. Over tea we had an unhurried discussion concerning the tuberculosis situation in Kien Tuong. We talked about setting up a B.C.G. immunization program in Kien Tuong and most importantly, we were able to obtain from him a large supply of INH. This he gave us on the spot to carry back with us. It comes in tablet form and is the main medication for the treatment of tuberculosis. We had been identifying increasing numbers of people with tuberculosis in Moc Hoa and our supplies were running thin. We were having difficulty obtaining it from other sources, so this was a major accomplishment for us and made all of our gallivanting about worthwhile.

Sunday 13 November

WHITE COLLAR SNIPER

During this time in Saigon, Williams and I may have had a close call. We had just finished eating on the roof restaurant of a large hotel on Tu Do Street and were set to return to the USAID guest house when a heavy rain began. We tried for half an hour to find an empty cab, but all were occupied. We walked one-and-a-half blocks from the hotel along a busy street running across Tu Do, but still could not get a cab. All the while the rain continued to pelt down. So we waited at the entrance of a shop. We waited about ten minutes.

I noted a woman standing in an office on the second floor of a building across the street. She brought a well-dressed man to the window and they looked at us. Apparently, they did not note that I was watching them also. The man opened a door on the second floor to a small porch on the front of the building and stretched straight his right arm, pointing at us with what I thought looked like a gun in his hand. I yelled at Willie to jump back, and I stepped quickly back into the store and cautiously looked around the corner of a window at them. The man lowered his hand and went back inside. Had we not noticed him and he shot at us, he could have easily escaped with the shot being muffled by the pouring rain. I had my .38 along though, and we saw him.

From sports I have an aggressive streak in me at times. If attacked, I will fight back. In high school I used to pitch baseball and got a kick out of striking batters out. It was me against them. I had a moving fastball and different good curve balls. With two strikes on a batter sometimes I'd start the curve out at the batter's head. It would break sharp and late and down across the plate. He would see it coming, aimed between his eyes and almost always either back away from the plate and have a third strike called or he'd take a swing at it and miss by a foot.

Sometimes a good offense is the best defense. The situation here seemed to be that a Vietnamese office worker, obviously a Communist sympathizer, spotted two Americans stuck in a driving rain and thought he would have some fun at their expense. If he had shot, I would have returned the favor and shot back. If he would have ducked back in, I was going to run across the street while shooting another round into his window and then maybe run up the inner stairway and send a few more through his office door to keep him entertained. Then I'd go back down and get out of there. He didn't shoot so none of this happened and I told Willie that we should get out of there, which we did.

SNAKE

Last night after the movie in the mess hall, as one of the Special Forces men was leaving through the door, he noticed a motion by his foot. He reached down and a snake bit him in the forearm. He was taken to the compound medical shack and seen by a Special Forces' medic. The sergeant major, who was drunk as a skunk, told the medic that he felt that the snake was not poisonous. The man was ten yards in front of me as he was leaving the door, and I had briefly seen the snake and thought it possible it could be a viper. I thought it best to proceed and give the antivenin for viper which was available in the shack. The medic didn't seem eager to do that and the sergeant major told me I was interfering. It was he who was interfering. I got mad, turned around and started to quickly walk away. Higgins, who was observing the scene, then ran and grabbed me and told me that it was my duty to go back, that I was the most qualified person to assess the matter and that it would be improper for me to back down. I agreed and went back and gave the antivenin. By this time the man who was bitten was considerably shaken by the situation.

Sunday 13 November continued

Earlier in the day Colonel F. decided to move the rest of my team back to the B-Compound. He needed more men for guard duty since the present guards had left and had not been replaced. There had also been disputes about minor disciplinary matters. I could understand a certain amount of this kind of thing, but our unit has its own sergeants and my men are to be generally disciplined by our personnel, not theirs. Now with the shack incident, it was one of their men who was clearly out of line. The next day at the 6 p.m. briefing I let them know how I felt about what happened with the shack episode and was quite vehement about it. The colonel didn't appreciate my side of the argument and had to stick up for his man. Douglass, in Can Tho, assured me that as he could see it, I was correct in the matter. Since I have returned, both the colonel and the sergeant major have been courteous and as a few days progressed, relations between us have improved a good measure.

They transferred Marachek out to another area in the Delta today. I wonder if he got into some sort of difficulty with the powers here.

14 November

Captain Jones had another close call in a helicopter today. Two weeks ago the chopper he was in was hit in the fuel tank and was forced to land. Today the pilot of the chopper he was in was hit in the elbow by a bullet. The copter was 30 feet off the ground when the pilot lost control and it nosed toward the ground. He regained control five feet off the ground and then the gunner took over the controls.

Last night at midnight we heard mortar rounds begin to fall about a mile and a half away and much machine-gun fire. One of the four bridges down the road was being hit. These are usually protected by ten Regional Force soldiers who live there with their families. The alert sounded at our compound and I was quite concerned that we were going to be hit. There was intermittent machine-gun fire from closeby — just a few blocks away. At 5 a.m. we began to receive the casualties. Two infants were brought in, each of whose parents had been killed. There were two women with bullet wounds of the abdomen and four or five soldiers with various wounds. These were taken care of by 10 a.m.

Then they began to fly in helicopter loads of wounded Vietnamese soldiers from A-Camp 414 who were in an operation near Cambodia. They ran into VC who were in well fortified positions. The company was hit with heavy casualties. Throughout the afternoon seven dead were brought in and 20 or so others with chest and abdominal injuries. Two Americans from the A-Camp were killed (there are only seven Americans there). My men had known these men well. One had been shot through the forehead; another American had been wounded in the leg. The helicopter pilot I mentioned before also came in at that time. We were able to do several abdominal cases, but then were overwhelmed and had to evacuate the rest of the severely injured to Can Tho.

18 November

Things have settled down. For the past two days we've been moving materials out of the Vietnamese storeroom/pharmacy which we hadn't gotten into previously. We had two separate pharmacies and this was not right — we needed to combine them. There were about 15 large crates piled one on another, the contents of which were not known to the Vietnamese stockroom worker or anyone else. These we cleared out and checked. The entire place was filthy, with lizards behind things and cockroaches under every box. There were certain large stocks of things we thought we did not have and needed badly. There was a very thick layer of dust on all shelves and bottles, and in the back was a large stock of obsolete French medication. We're going to take all these things out, clean and paint the place and then return the usable stock combined with our supply to make one pharmacy.

The X-ray machine has been non-functional for two days and this has put a crimp in my TB detection program. I hope it will be running again within two weeks.

19 November

Today I received a telegram. "Message to Captain Kammholz MILPHAP Daughter Heidi Beth Born 0122 Hours At Milwaukee Lutheran Hosp Wisconsin on 19 Nov 66 Weight 5 lbs 6 Oz Length 18.5" Mother and Daughter Are Doing Fine Congratulations"

20 November

Captain M. and his airboats [73-c] were back in action. On the day before they had come across a suspicious area in a tree line. The boats lined up, fired in turn at the area and a secondary explosion occurred. On the second pass Captain M. noted a bunker still partially under water, and two VC were trying to get into it. In their haste, they became jammed in the entryway with their buttocks and legs sticking out. Captain M. opened up on them with his machine gun. On one occasion during the day, the airboats were moving quite fast and Captain M. was thrown five feet out of the boat when it hit a rough spot.

21 November

There have been some interesting operations here the past two days. The Navy has brought in three hovercraft [73-a, b]. These are 25 yards long and 15 yards wide. They are boat-type craft with a large propeller on the bottom like a rotary power mower which creates air pressure beneath and lifts the craft three to four feet off the ground. There is a large propeller on the back which moves the craft forward, and it can go up to 60 miles per hour. On the boat is a .50-caliber machine gun and several smaller machine guns. Today helicopters, the airboats, these three hovercraft and a few ground companies went into an area near the place where they recently ran into trouble. Last week, as I had described, they ran into enemy-fortified positions. One airboat was caught and two Americans in it were killed and about 35 Vietnamese troops received injuries and eight VN troops were killed.

The helicopters arrived in the area first and began putting machine-gun fire into the small village (15 hits). The VC were in the village and began to leave

and head out toward the Cambodian border. The airboats with Captain M. then arrived on the scene as did the hovercraft which moved to the flanks of the operation and began pouring .50-caliber shells into the village, causing more VC to leave. Captain M. and his five airboats, moving in line formation, caught up with 18 VC retreating along a canal and gunned them down. The boats came at them in a line. The lead boat opened up and then turned in a circle and came back following the fifth boat. The others did likewise, making a circle, and were able to keep continuous fire on the target by this formation, each boat firing in turn. One VC raised both his hands as if to surrender, but when the airboat approached he grabbed for a rifle a U.S. medic was holding. Captain M. let him have it with the M-16, stitching bullets from his waist up to his head. The M-16 round through the head caused his brain to explode like a grenade.

All told they got 56 confirmed VC killed. They captured the 40-horsepower motor that the VC unit had captured from us in the operation last week. This was the same VC unit that had killed the two Americans, eight Vietnamese and caused 35 Vietnamese casualties a week ago. So the score was even. The village that was hit though may have been inside Cambodia. The village first was flying a VC flag. When the hovercraft began putting .50 caliber shells into it, the VC flag was taken down and the Cambodian flag was raised. Thus, this might turn into a border incident. This was the VC unit that had blown several bridges. Captured documents told of an operation planned to destroy the district barge.

22 November

I was talking tonight in the bar with Dr. Harper, our new Project Vietnam surgeon, who has been here a few weeks. His motives for coming are apparently adventure and to get away from the routine at home. He has been in general practice six years in partnership with a surgeon and internist in Oklahoma. He lives near the Osage reservation. All the Osages are wealthy due to extensive oil deposits on their land. Harper owns a large tract of land just outside his small town. The oil on the land belongs to the Indians and Harper has two wells, but the wheat he grows is his. Also, a highway is planned through his land and any money to be gained from this happenstance will be his, not the Indians' — a strange arrangement. Dr. Harper is a somewhat quiet, but easy-going fellow. He raises orchids in his greenhouse in Oklahoma,

53-a   Bar in B-41 club with souvenirs adorning the walls.

53-b   Some of our team and two VN counterparts. From left, back: Brown, Nelson; middle: McCurley, Williams, Boyle; front: Myself, Dr. Farber, Song, Henderson, Nguyen.

53-c   Song and children.

53-d   Nelson and Higgins.

53-e   Me with Charley.

53-f   Dr. Ting

53-g   Ting's daughters.

53-h   Nguyen and Jackson in lab.

54-a   Duck hunt. From left: Barton, Ting, Fong, myself, driver.

54-b   Me with shotgun and egret.

54-c   Fong and helper with adjutant stork.

54-d   Moc Hoa at height of flood.

54-e   Chopper view of Moc Hoa flood.

54-f   Marketplace at Moc Hoa.

54-g   Explosion of 55-gallon fuel drum.

54-h   Rub-a-dub-dub, three boys in a 55-gallon drum.

54-i   Site of explosion.

55-a Walking from B-41 to the hospital.
From left: Sgt. Brown, Nelson, myself, Kelly.

55-b Anesthetist's ride home.
Katherine Gallager in sampan.

55-c Patients arriving for clinic.

55-d Transporting patient from surgery to ward.
From left: patient, Song, Higgins, Boyle McCurley, Dr. Taylor.

55-f Plane airdropping supplies during flood. The supply package went through the roof of the first brown roofed building. No one was hurt.

55-e Immunizing at school building. Standing from left: Jerry Walsh, patient, McCurley.

55-g Cobras at gate of B-41.

56-a Leaving the briefing. General Westmoreland at left and Colonel Fernandes.

56-b Chopper view of Ap Bac.

56-c View from helicopter at Long Kot.

56-d USAID chopper.

56-e At Long Kot. Nguyen, district chief, myself.

56-f Boys with water buffalo.

56-g A-Camp 415 Tuyen Nhon during flood.

56-h Girl in sampan.

hunts antelope each year in Colorado and fishes each spring in Minnesota. I spent three hours talking with him in the bar about these things over a few Bier Larue.

27 November

Captain M. with his "Mike Force" — Chinese Nung troops — went on an operation with the hovercraft a few days ago. Our hospital received a VC who had been shot in the hand and an 18-month-old child whose parents had been killed. One of our nurses adopted him temporarily, but later he will be picked up and taken care of by an aunt.

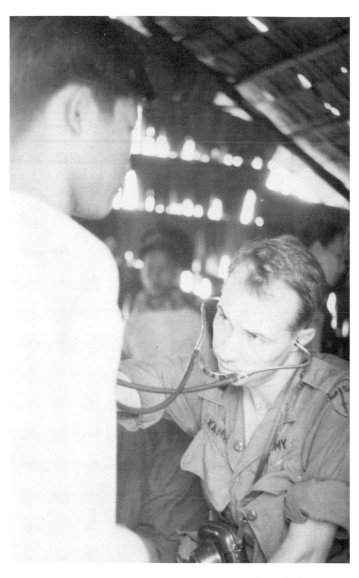

Myself on medical patrol listening to a Chieu Hoi. This man had a healed bullet wound through the chest. He was probably a former VC who had moved out of VC territory during the flood.

Canal scene.

Hitch hiking a ride near Nhon Ninh.

29 November

AP BAC

Dr. Ting, Higgins, Brown and I took a chopper to Ap Bac [73-d, e, f], which is in our province to the southeast of Moc Hoa, to see patients there and also to see refugees down the canal between Ap Bac and Kien Quan II. We set up to see the refugees in a grass hut [73-g].

Grass huts are perfectly functional in the tropics. They blend in with their environment and after they have lived out their usefulness, they return to the soil without polluting it. They can be built quickly by their occupants with mainly labor and little requirement for money. They are cooler than a more permanent structure and allow air to circulate better. People who live in them aren't as likely to have allergies to things inside them such as is common in the northern climate permanent structures. Certain things are relatively free in the tropics; housing is one of them. Neither are there any heating bills in the winter. Rice grows readily in the Delta and there is a sufficiency of fruit, fish and fowl. With the right clothing, the climate is bearable and can even be enjoyed many times. The main problems are disease and war, otherwise this place isn't so bad. The children in the countryside all have smiles.

In the afternoon we had some time to sit around and discuss miscellaneous odds and ends. A year ago Dr. Ting was stationed in the more mountainous region of the country. This was early in the war. He and some Vietnamese troops were out one day with a fairly newly arrived U.S. unit. A village chief whom he knew approached to greet them. The village chief spoke only a little English. He was dressed in black — as many Vietnamese do — but the leader of the U.S. unit, thinking that this was a sign that he was VC, called out "VC?". The chief answered OK and he was immediately shot down.

There is a small mountain which one can see to the north from here across Cambodia in Tay Ninh. On the top of it is a Special Forces camp. On the bottom is the only well in the area. The Special Forces use the well three days each week and the VC use it four days. There is an unspoken agreement that this is a neutral area.

During the flood at Ap Bac the latrine at the small compound where three or four U.S. personnel stay went out. So in order to relieve themselves, they would have to get in a sampan (the compound was adjacent to the canal) and hang their butts over the side. The Vietnamese troops in the area would post a guard on the main bridge about two blocks away and watch for just such an occasion. When someone got in the sampan, the guard would sound the alert and the whole VN company and some townspeople would come running onto the bridge shouting and banging pots and kettles just to get the man's goat. They apparently got quite a bang out of seeing an American do something which to them is an everyday normal occurrence.

One sees the Vietnamese squatting all over having bowel movements. No more than 20 feet out the back window of my room in the compound is another building which houses some important Vietnamese townspeople. If one were up early enough in the morning during the flood, one might be greeted by a glimpse of the lady of the house to the back of the billets balancing on the windowsill with her behind hanging to the outside. Every day you could see the kids all over out in the open doing this, and it was especially amusing when they would perch themselves on a fence. So, there were special problems during the flood. Most of the time the VN would go out some distance when relieving themselves. The absence of temperate climate plumbing did allow hookworm, roundworm and other parasites to flourish. At least none of the toddlers were bothered by diaper rash.

Ap Bac has a population of about 1,500. It is located at the crossing of two large canals over which there are two large bridges, the most prominent features of the town.

The clinic there has about the floor space of a one-car garage, though it is longer and narrower. In one room the midwife lives. The other three small rooms are for treatment. All of the rooms were so filthy that I believe no one had ever washed or dusted anything off. The cabinets and shelves were filthy.

The health worker there had been reported to have been selling the antibiotics that we had given him during the flood. Dr. Ting wasn't sure or not if he was selling them, but at the least he was very lazy and few of the townspeople would go to see him. We decided to send him to Moc Hoa where we could watch him and put Kwan at Ap Bac in his place. Mr. Kwan is a surgery nurse whom I have been using during the total absence of other interpreters during the flood. It is better to use him as a replacement than to have no one as a replacement. He is intelligent and a nice fellow.

Higgins liked Ap Bac and I decided that in a few weeks I would put Higgins and Williams at Ap Bac.

The next day we set up in the clinic in Ap Bac and were again inundated by patients — 246 of them. Dr. Ting and I saw the patients. Higgins spent most of the day pulling teeth. The following day Ting left, and we stayed in Ap Bac and saw 115 patients.

KIEN QUAN II

A helicopter was to take one of the other Americans at Ap Bac to Kien Quan II [74-b], and I decided that we should go along and see what people we could see. When we arrived the next day, we found that there was no interpreter and so we called Moc Hoa and were lucky to get a chopper to bring Mr. Kwan and Nguyen down to Kien Quan that afternoon. The town is only six blocks down the canal from the A-Camp, and we set up immunizations and sick call and saw 111 in one afternoon.

The village chief invited us to dinner and quite a dinner that was! We had catfish fried with the head on. The eyes seemed a special delicacy to the Vietnamese so I let them have them. The next thing to be served looked like french fries, but were actually minnows. I was told by Higgins that they were good so I tried one. To my surprise, they were very tasty and I ate a dozen of them.

That evening we had another dinner, this time with the LLDB (the seven or eight Vietnamese Special Forces people at the A-Camp). The LLDB are the Vietnamese counterparts to the U.S. Special Forces and they command the CIDG (Civilian Irregular Defense Group) forces of the camp. It got to be a drinking party where the glasses of a U.S. and Vietnamese would be filled with beer and then they would see who could drink it the fastest.

The next day was Sunday and I wanted to go out and treat some people, but the Vietnamese didn't want to go and said we should go Monday. So Monday, seven Vietnamese guards, the four of us and a Special Forces' medic, Sergeant Garcia [74-e], got into a boat and were about to go two kilometers up a canal to Buc Hoa, toward Moc Hoa. On starting the engine the propeller got tangled in barbed wire and we had a half-hour delay getting it untangled. One of the VN soldiers tried talking me into giving him my banana clip (30-round clip) for his 20-round clip. He was a good fellow and we kidded around a bit.

Finally we got going up the canal [74-a]. It was a hot, humid day, without a breeze. The heavy heat

draped over us as the boat sliced slowly through it. We went up the narrow canal for quite a few miles. It was marsh terrain with no trees and we could be heard coming from a long distance away. Therefore, I was quite concerned about getting ambushed. The others were not. Two VC in the heavy brush on either side of the canal could have easily wiped out the whole boatload of us.

The health clinic in Buc Hoa [74-c, d] had only a midwife. We set up there and saw 239 patients in a hectic day. Hectic mainly because of three loud-mouthed Vietnamese. One was the village police chief, another a soldier keeping the people in line and a third a VN lieutenant directing people. They were all no more than ten feet away and kept screaming and hollering at the people. I was reluctant to tell them to be quiet since two of them were village officials. Before the day was out, the police chief had pilfered a bottle or so of our medicine and one of the guards stole two banana clips from Brown. While there we were served a meal with an especially flavorful *nuoc mam* (nook mom), a fish sauce which was quite good.

That night we talked about going the other way up the canal, but the Special Forces medic said we would need two boats, because with one we might be easily ambushed. This worried me and I decided that we would cancel that trip and head back to Moc Hoa. Without security one is quite unnecessarily risking his neck, and our job anyway was to set up permanent health stations rather than make hit and miss trips here and there. I decided that Higgins and Williams would go to Ap Bac and two others later to Kien Quan II at 416.

8 December

PIT VIPER

Killed a snake tonight. We were watching a Japanese Frankenstein horror movie in the mess hall. It was raining out and at the end when the first man walked out the door, a four-foot snake came flying in through the door just as it was opened. It struck at Jeff, the USAID assistant province representative. It hit his leather shoe but did not penetrate. Someone hit it over the head and stunned it and then they put it outside in a ditch where it floated down to a larger ditch. I wasn't sure it was dead. Someone got a flashlight and I got a sickle, and I picked it out of the ditch with the sickle. It wasn't dead. I jabbed it in the head with the sickle and held it while Jeff cut its head off with his pocket knife. It was a pit viper.

15 December

OPIUM

Yesterday Ong Song was telling me what his daughter, who works at USAID, had discovered. A package was put on a USAID helicopter by the province chief; another Vietnamese was carrying it. It came open and Art Elmore and Song's daughter saw that it contained a huge quantity of opium. Song tells that a Vietnamese general, in addition to the province chief, is involved in transporting this opium. I was at the USAID house tonight and Art mentioned what a good job, in general, the province chief was doing. Then Harper said, ''outside of opium smuggling.'' Art related that though he did not like this, he felt that he would nevertheless attempt to continue his relations and work with the province chief as though this did not exist. He said that the Vietnamese people rather expect that the officials engage in such practices and do not consider it morally wrong. The province chief is aware that Art knows of his involvement in this opium transportation. I have heard that there may possibly be an investigation of this in the making.

15 December continued

Art was telling about the 1958 rebellion in Indonesia. We had advisors on both the government and the rebel sides, and these men knew each other. The idea of this was that whatever side won, we would have been advising the winning side.

I just had to go to the hospital to sew a laceration above the eye.

Things at the hospital are changing. The old storeroom next to the medical ward has now been cleaned out and the shelves repainted, and is shaping up to be a decent pharmacy. We've gotten some large shelves and placed them in the future post-op room in the surgical building, and this is shaping up to be a decent warehouse. The Chieu Hoi have been putting fill in the hospital grounds. Two days ago I placed Higgins and Williams at the dispensary in Ap Bac. Tomorrow, Brown and Kelly will be going to Tuyen Nhon, the chief town of another district, to work in the dispensary there. They are eager to go. They will have to make decisions on their own and will have a lot more responsibility than they would have here.

The CIDG in Bien Hiep, which is on the Cambodian border, made a deal with the Cambodians to pay 100,000 p ($1,000) for cigarettes and food. They got these things, but then refused to pay the Cambodians.

Kien Quan II was mortared tonight, eight rounds fell in the compound. I had been in Kien Quan II two weeks ago.

Ten p.m. We just received a man with a bullet in his chest. He was hit at 2 p.m. and came 20 kilometers to get here. We put in a chest tube and got a lot of blood and air out. We gave him a unit of blood we had and drew another from his daughter and gave him that also. He's most likely VC.

18 December

Six were injured slightly in the attack at Kien Quan last night. This was only a diversionary attack, however. Radio contact was lost with a forward ambush patrol. The next morning they discovered 14 of this 26-man patrol had been killed. Six wounded stragglers came in later. The VN patrol had taken the same route every day for two weeks. A well-setup VC ambush was waiting and cut them apart. By the way, today is the VC celebration of the anniversary of the National Liberation Front.

Today I had a discussion about the war with one of the local Vietnamese. I asked if he thought increased bombing would end the war. He replied that we must invade the North. I asked if he thought then that China would come in. He said yes, and that we must then bomb China. I asked if he thought Russia would then come in. He said no. I asked how many people in Moc Hoa would like to see the VC win. He said many of those who were not refugees, especially the uneducated ones. With them, he said, the VC propaganda was very effective. I asked if he thought that these people thought that the U.S. was like France and would like to take over this country. He said that yes, they think this.

On a map at the B-Team here this province capital, Moc Hoa, where we are, is considered to be ''pacified'' yet how can this be if many of the people would like the VC to win. I asked if he thought that the pacification programs would be effective. He said that he could not answer that.

A few days ago Dai uy Fong exploded several large water mines up the river. These were captured mines. He got a good haul of fish from these explosions. His information network alerted him that the VC were bringing the mines down the river in a large sampan. When the VC got down here with them, he and his men were waiting and killed one of the VC. The others escaped, but he then captured these water mines. He's quite an energetic person. A few days ago he got three VC suspects in town out of bed at 3 a.m. and began interrogating them.

27 December

Dai uy Fong received a rifle scope from one of the A-Teams. He intends to wait near the Cambodian border and get a VC tax collector with this.

Last evening was spent at the club talking with Dr. Harper who left today for the U.S. Tom Hendricks, the commander of A-414 and Dr. Eggerstedt were also at the table. Eggerstedt is a military M.D. like myself. He is the first permanent replacement for the other M.D.'s who were supposed to be on this team. Tom told us of an incident that happened to him on December 2. He and several other Americans were out on an operation with the CIDG. They were attacking one target and two helicopters were attacking another target. The smoke got heavy and one of the helicopters shot some rockets into the cloud of smoke caused by the CIDG. One of the rockets hit one of the CIDG in the back and tore him in half. Ten of the CIDG became very angry and threatened to throw grenades at Tom. The rockets missed Tom by only a very short distance.

A similar incident had occurred to Captain Halley a few weeks ago. A helicopter mistook his group of CIDG for VC and fired the helicopter machine gun at them. He said that not ten yards in front of him the water was turned into a churning froth. He dove into a canal and was lucky to escape.

Tom told us about other things. The sergeant major here had caused another problem. Tom got infuriated and went to see the colonel, and told him that the sergeant major could go to hell as far as he was concerned.

Among other things, he stated that the province chief pays 500,000 p's each month to higher Viet officials to keep his job and that if he (Tom) were a Vietnamese, he would be on the VC side. He told how one day the CIDG had a VC suspect and his wife and children and tied up the suspect, and shot him in front of the wife and children.

My men and hospital personnel at province chief's Christmas dinner.

Christmas dinner at province chief's.

The day before Christmas Dr. Harper, Ting and I passed out Red Cross presents at the Chieu Hoi center and at the orphanage. On Christmas Eve the province chief threw a party, inviting 300 people. This was held at a school yard. They roasted five Cambodian cows. They didn't get them done, the meat was raw and about the toughest I've ever tried. There was entertainment with a small band and local singers. Hong, the interpreter from Ap Bac, sang. He was formerly a singer in Saigon. We left early to go to the last half of a party at Mr. Song's house [74-f]. He showed a movie about VC saboteurs in Saigon and their capture by police. This was a propaganda film and all in the film were actors. Sunday at 11 a.m. six of us went to Nguyen's home [74-g]. He has a small two-room area in a long building with a dirt floor. I gave Nguyen a present of a board game and this was played until lunch was served. He served a potato chip-like thing which was made from lobster meat and wrapped in rice paper. This was dipped in *nuoc mam*. We also had Bier Larue. Before the shrimp was served I had to leave to get back to the B-Camp to join the group who had been invited to the province chief's at 1 p.m. There I ate turkey, ham, cranberries, stuffing and drank German wine. I made the mistake of eating two servings. I then went back to Nguyen's, and he insisted that I eat some large shrimp. I spent the rest of the afternoon lying down because I couldn't sit up without being very uncomfortable. Now I know what a boa constrictor feels like when he swallows a pig.

(This was not the routine as far as the general meal situation was concerned. There was food enough, but usually there were things such as lukewarm sandwich-meat and rice. I remember a number of meals with ants, little red ones, crawling over the rice at the USAID house. When I arrived in Vietnam I was a bit overweight and when I got back to the U.S. my ribs were showing. I think the activity in the warm climate played a part. I had lost one sixth of my weight while in Vietnam.)

HELICOPTERS AND PLANES

Before coming to Vietnam I had been taken up in a helicopter by my neighbor in Fort Eustis, Virginia. I became airsick easily and while over the mothball fleet at Newport News I noticed that my legs were becoming cold and clammy and shortly I vomited on the glass bottom of the observation helicopter. I was ill for the rest of the afternoon.

On one helicopter trip out of Moc Hoa during the flood, for the first part of the flight the pilot flew only six-to-eight feet above ground and hopped over the tree lines as if we were doing hurdles. The pilot wouldn't have been able to do this at any time other than the flood because of sniper fire from just out of town. On arriving at the destination airport, he circled and proceeded to come in for a landing down the runway as if we were a light plane coming in.

On one flight in a Caribou we looked down and saw a village flying a VC flag. In a bit we heard a loud ping. We looked at each other as if to say, "What was that?" I thought at first it was something from the engine, but it must have been a bullet going through the fuselage.

One day Higgins told me that a chopper was going to land on the hospital grounds. Some U.S. casualties were lying wounded to the northwest. Usually they just bring the casualties in. I grabbed the emergency case and just before jumping into the helicopter asked Higgins and Henderson to come along. I knew they weren't afraid to come, but Higgins said, "Doc, you gotta go yourself." I would have ordered them to come if I had wanted. Something seemed fishy. With the recent episode between me and the sergeant major, I think the Special Forces wanted to see if I would go out of my way to help them in a jam. I think there were bets set up in the club with Higgins betting I would go alone. Anyway, by this time the helicopter was taking off. In my hurry to get into the helicopter I hadn't thought about strapping myself in the seat and as the helicopter was still climbing past the edge of town, I was kneeling on the floor checking things in the emergency case. I noticed my foot hanging out the side of the open door. I remember the helicopter tilting just slightly, and I looked down and realized that with any more tilt the emergency case and I would be out the side of the open door, freely falling a few hundred feet down through the warm, sunny day. There was mucky ground below and I fleetingly wondered if there might be a slim chance of being alive on hitting this. When I was a kid we used to jump off the garage roof to the soft ground below, but this was 20 times higher. I grabbed onto the edge of the seat and crawled away from the door and strapped myself in. Soon we were radioed that the pickup had been made and the casualties were being flown directly to Saigon. I never found out who these casualties were, and I still think the whole thing was a fake set-up that had been arranged because of a bet. If it was a bet, Higgins won.

Several times I was transported by an unusual Swiss airplane. It had a single engine and seating for only about a half-dozen people. Its main feature was the powerful engine with a very high rpm propeller. I believe the pitch of the propeller could be changed while it was rotating. We would sit vibrating without moving forward as the engine gradually revved up to a loud, high-pitched whine. Only then would the plane start forward and taxi a very short distance before taking off. Once off, it climbed quickly in a fairly tight, upward spiral. The advantage to this in Switzerland was that only a short runway would be needed in the mountainous terrain. The advantage here was the avoidance of sniper fire from outside the runway. On landing, the plane descended in a similar tight spiral. Other light planes came in this way to some degree also. A plane would arrive high over the runway without any prior descent and then go into the downward spiral, providing an interesting landing.

Boarding airplane.

One day I had boarded a light plane for a trip to Can Tho and had stopped at Me Tho to change planes. There I was told that a few days earlier a similar plane had landed. A Vietnamese in suit and tie walked in haste to the front of this plane, into the path of the propeller and was beheaded.

12 January

I haven't written for some time and so will have to catch up a bit with things. Another Special Forces man was killed several weeks ago. The VC had booby trapped a forward operating base with grenades. He was picking these grenades up and throwing them. This was OK for the first grenade, but the fuse on the second was short, a clever trick, and it exploded before he threw it.

One week ago Cates (Shotgun, as he is called) — the small spotter airplane pilot here — caught three rounds in the cockpit. Cates received a superficial wound in the neck. An air strike was called in on the house from which the fire came. A thousand-pound bomb made a direct hit on the hut.

One week ago a sergeant came in from BTT (Binh Than Thuy). He had been ill for a day with high fever, headache and muscle pains. We did a malaria smear and found none, and the symptoms were not enough to tell me what the illness was, so we sent him to Saigon. Several days later I received a call from the medic in BTT that ten Vietnamese who had trained recently with the sergeant in the northern part of the country had become ill with fever, headache and muscle aches. I told the medic that I would call the Third Field Hospital to find out what the diagnosis had been on the sergeant we sent in a few days earlier. The next day I received word that the diagnosis was fever of unknown origin and that his condition was unchanged. I then called the medic at BTT. He told me that eight more men had come down with the illness and that all were quite ill now, with temperatures to 104 and 105. I told him that I thought this might be scrub typhus and to start these people on tetracycline. Several days later the men were all improved and nearly well. I then relayed a message to the Third Field Hospital in Saigon telling them that these men who had trained with the sergeant had likely scrub typhus and that they had responded to tetracycline. The medic in BTT had noted escars on quite a few of the men. An escar is a scab at the site of the mite bite and is a helpful diagnostic sign in scrub typhus.

Two days ago Dr. Ting and I flew to Tuyen Nhon. We had Kelly fly back because a new X-ray unit arrived at Moc Hoa. Brown had set it up in one half of a Chieu Hoi building and it was functioning well. Helping him were the CIDG medic-interpreter and two hamlet health workers.

Today, I found out that the people here were going to pull the interpreter out of Ap Bac that our team had been using for half of each day. This man was here during New Year's and sang at the province chief's party. He was a former singer from Saigon and the rumor is that they want him back here to sing at their parties. If he leaves Ap Bac, I'll have to pull my men out of there. So, because the province chief wants a singer at his parties, the people at Ap Bac will be left without adequate health care.

14 January

There was an operation today down in the Pocket with 30 helicopters [75-a] and a few hundred troops. They killed 50 VC and captured three. We got one who was shot through both legs. We received three injured friendlies, one with an eye injury, another with a broken ankle and a third with two bullet wounds to the leg and a broken leg. One ten-year-old boy was brought in from a VC area. He had been hit by rocket fragments two days ago and died of infection a few minutes after arriving in the hospital.

20 January

I'd like to talk about the hamlet health worker program for a while. Formerly these workers were trained by each A-Team medic. Now, they've centralized the training and they are trained in Can Tho by a Special Forces medic and by the hospital in Can Tho. According to Dr. Ting, last year we had a sufficient number of these health workers in the province, but the pay was too low and most left for other jobs. They were paid 2,000 piasters per month (about $18 per month). Dr. Ting feels that if they could be paid 3,000 p/month they would stay. Last month the A-Team at Tuyen Nhon had eight of these health workers trained in Can Tho. Special Forces are allowed to pay them 1,500 p/month for six months. Before the six months are up, the Ministry of Health is supposed

to take over the pay. These eight have finished their training and are now working with my team in Tuyen Nhon, and two of them are at our hospital for two weeks of further training. After six weeks they are to be placed in the hamlets. None of the other three districts have sent any hamlet workers to the course, although there are still a few workers in each district. Today, the Special Forces medic in charge of the training program paid us a visit and told me that out of the whole Fourth Corps, only three workers were sent to him to be trained. The team at Kien Quan II managed to find one candidate. That district needs at least six. We went down to the hospital and talked to Mr. Song to see if he would know of anyone we could train.

He brought over seven of our "student nurses." I never was sure what the situation with these people was. Apparently they were working virtually without pay at our hospital to learn some nursing skills. They all seemed quite excited about the prospect of being able to go to Can Tho. So these will be trained as hamlet health workers. Most of them, according to Ong Song, come from hamlets near Moc Hoa. So, we hope things will work out well for them.

Four days ago Dr. Marsh, an assistant of Dr. Douglass, visited us. He is to be in charge of Rural Health and is new at the job. I had met him in San Antonio before we came over.

The following day, Colonel Eisner, the MACV surgeon, with two aides, toured our hospital. Colonel Eisner is, in essence, in charge of the entire medical program in Vietnam. He was quite pleased with how things were coming at the hospital.

The next day Dr. Phelps visited. He is in charge of the "Volunteer Physicians for Vietnam" project — the civilian M.D.'s who spend two months in Vietnam.

I found out more today about the opium smuggling going on. The province chief and everyone on down in his office is involved. About 13 kilograms of it passed through Moc Hoa this month. It's worth 13,000 p/kilo. The police chief was investigating this and the province chief told him to lay off the investigation, which he did.

The province chief recently made a quick $500. He sold some captured VC ammunition to Go Long Province for fireworks for Tet.

It had been said that a restaurant owner downtown made a payoff to the province chief so that he could collect taxes from the Moc Hoa market area.

There is a drug store downtown that has been involved in selling drugs to the VC.

**Province chief's meeting —
USAID's Jeff Harris on left.**

28 January

Ong Vuong, one of our two interpreters, is going to leave for Saigon and likely will not return because of his father's insistence that he not live in this town. A month or so ago a CIDG trooper pulled a gun on both my interpreters and told them to move out of a certain house. I asked Vuong about the thing Dr. Ting had told me of having to make a payoff in order to obtain a job. He said it was true. The Vietnamese worker in the USAID office in charge of hiring interpreters asked indirectly to be paid off for procuring a job. The amount needed to be paid for a good job or a job at all ranged from $50 to $100 plus. I've told this to the USAID people here and an investigation has been started.

29 January

There was a large operation today; 500 CIDG and RF/PF (Regional Forces/Popular Forces) were lifted by helicopter into a VC area. All the homes were empty, not even women and children were present. In one place fish were being cooked over an open fire, but no one could be found in the area. The operation had been planned for some time and coordination had been made with the VN air force. So obviously, the VC had prior notice that the operation was coming.

24 January

The most recent "Volunteer for Vietnam Surgeon," who has been here three weeks now, suggested that we put an M.D. and an enlisted man at the hospital throughout the night. The hospital is at the edge of town and unprotected. If the need arises during the night, we arm ourselves, get in the jeeps, go down and take care of the problem. So we are on duty and available, but our constant presence at night is not only unnecessary but extremely dangerous. At present, the Special Forces do not allow men out of the compound after 7 p.m. except on official business for security reasons. It would be a perfect set-up without guards down there for a terrorist attack on these men and I refused to consider the idea. There were a lot of other things that he thought should be done according to his notions, many of which I considered to be impractical and likely to cause a deterioration in our good rapport with the Vietnamese hospital personnel. I had a meeting with him and Ting and told him what I thought of this. Before this we had been on reasonably friendly terms. His medical effort was much appreciated. His attempt to usurp command was not. Nothing like having someone who will be here only two months try to take over command, cause a reversal in relationships and lay down rules for all to follow after he has left.

More about the CIDG from Ong Vuong and Binh with whom Eggerstedt and I had dinner today down in the market. The CIDG are greatly disliked by the local people. The local police are afraid of them and will not enforce the law upon them. All the stores are closed after 8 p.m. because various owners had been threatened by the CIDG and asked to give money to individual CIDG when they lose in their gambling or at other times. In one instance in another district the CIDG stopped a barge with a police escort carrying supplies. The police were threatened, and the CIDG took a portion of the cargo and then released them. Thus, the CIDG have a free hand to harass the people if they wish, and they often do.

I was told several days ago that all the people know of most of the dishonesty and corruption of the local government and this, together with the CIDG behavior, creates no enthusiasm for the present government. Some of the CIDG though are VC and function in ways to discredit the CIDG.

1 February

The salary for each CIDG camp is $20,000 per month, and there are four such camps in this province.

McGrath has had a portion of his Counter Terror (CT) platoon [75-b] out for the past three days. He had found out that four VC were making regular trips into a village near the border each day. One man on the CT platoon was from that village and the villagers told him that these VC were not paying certain of their debts. A 14-man group was sent out and they went out at 3 a.m. each day for three days to set up an ambush for when the VC would approach the village. The third day the four VC were spotted in camouflaged hats. The CT men called out to them to surrender, but they started firing and so the CT opened up and killed three and sank their sampan.

Tet is nearly here [75-e]. I can hardly believe it, but the people are actually cleaning up the garbage that has been lying around for months and they are painting their shops. All the stores have fancy candies and cookies and firecrackers. Dr. Ting left for Saigon for two weeks to celebrate Tet, and the hospital will be half-staffed for the next two weeks.

Ong Song's daughter was married and our team was invited to the wedding [75-c].

2 February

We discovered TB in one of the orphans and recently have been taking X-rays on the rest of them. There are about 30 orphans in all. One of them started crying and we couldn't figure out what he was upset about. Our interpreter asked him why, and then we began to laugh at the answer. The child had told him that he was afraid of the black American — Kelly — our X-ray tech.

(I have lost contact with most of the men, but Kelly has called on and off over the years to wish me a Merry Christmas. In order to keep his brother from being drafted, Kelly volunteered for two subsequent tours in Vietnam, exposing himself to great danger.)

In front of TB ward. Interpreter on left. Two TB patients are to my right and left. The man to my left was very faithful in taking his medicine and appreciative of his treatment.

TUBERCULOSIS

After several months "in country," one day I reflected upon what were some of the main health problems and what I could do to affect them. It seemed that TB was one of the most prevalent of diseases and was probably, outside of the war, the main cause of death in the land. I set about to see what could be done. Before the flood, the end room of the medical ward held about a dozen TB patients. Dr. Ting and the VN nurses were mainly involved in their care. The patients received shots of streptomycin, but many were not on INH at all. INH and streptomycin were the standard treatment at the time, with INH being the most important of the two. Streptomycin alone was not very good treatment. INH was the drug that was responsible for the emptying out and eventual closing down of the tuberculosis hospitals throughout the U.S.

Just as we were getting things organized and getting everybody educated on the importance of the INH, the flood came. The TB patients left the ward for other parts and after the flood only a few returned.

X-ray had not been available before we arrived. I set up an office [93-d] in the room next to X-ray and each day we saw a batch of people with chronic *hoa* (cough). The window ledge behind me was about eight feet from the ground and was located in a part of the hospital where someone could come up un-

A picturesque old man who had come
in from the countryside.

tion. Others, after receiving treatment for several months and improving, often discontinued their treatment in spite of having been told that they could expect to improve initially, but that they must not discontinue therapy until being told to so.

One day a little boy [76-d] of about ten, who was living in the Catholic orphanage, came to us. He was edematous and had a chronic cough. His chest X-ray showed extensive TB. I felt that he probably didn't have much time to live when he came in, but after some months on treatment he was vigorous and healthy looking.

I remember a middle-aged man who came in from far out in the countryside. He initially was very ill and stayed on the ward. He stayed on the ward a long time and there was a great improvement in his condition. I remember him standing and looking at us a few days before we were ready to go back to the States. I wonder what went through his mind? I think he was uneasy and sensed that we were leaving. I knew he appreciated our having been there.

VACUUM GLASSES

These were short, bulbous bottles. The Vietnamese would heat the base and apply the mouth to the patient's skin, often over the back. As the base cooled, a vacuum formed. Then, when the bottle was pulled off, there remained about a two-inch diameter reddish circle where the vacuum had affected the skin.

They did this particularly for patients with infections. Since there didn't seem to be any great harm in it, we didn't try to stop them from doing it. Likely they wouldn't have listened to us anyway. Perhaps, though I really didn't think so, there even could have been something helpful to it. Maybe in some way this was a non-specific stimulus to the immune system. Anyway, it was entertaining to see and was undoubtedly psychologically beneficial to the patient. It gave the relatives something to do and gave them a feeling of helping.

PATIENTS

We had some interesting patients at the hospital. One was called Hoot-toot-ra-phoot [76-a]. We called him this because one time he came up to me and said this repeatedly before I could get our interpreter to help me out. Hoot had a fondness for plain phenergan

noticed. I made plans what to do if a grenade were thrown in the window.

A total of 183 patients with TB were detected between August of 1966 and April of 67. A few were placed on the ward if they were bad enough or from out of town and willing to stay. Others were given INH and would come to the hospital for streptomycin shots during the week. Careful records were made to follow their reliability of receiving medication and I made a map of the town and province with colored pins marking the patient's home location. I became known as *Bac-Si-Lau* (TB). After a while we began to have problems with the INH supply, and Dr. Ting and I had to make a trip to the main TB hospital in Saigon to get a larger supply. About half of the patients were fairly reliable in receiving their medica-

(a cough medicine without codeine). He didn't have TB, but every so often he would go to the outpatient department and they would give him a dose or two for cough. One day they ran out and gave him some pills instead. Hoot took the pills and flung them across the room. Thereafter we tried to keep some phenergan in stock just in case he would come in so as not to disappoint him.

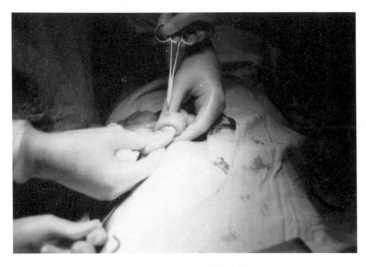

This is an intussusception of the bowel (a folding over of the bowel within itself). It was undoubtedly related to the large amount of ascaris worms that were found in his intestine.

This man had both hands blown off and was blinded by a booby trap. He is mentioned in October 17 note.

One time there was a patient with an intussusception of the bowel (a folding over of the bowel within itself). It was undoubtedly related to the large amount of ascaris worms that were found in his intestine.

Another patient had both hands blown off and was blinded by a booby trap. This is the casualty mentioned in the note of 17 October.

On one occasion a boy [76-c] from far out in the countryside was given some medicine by his parent. We think he might have been given an excessive amount of ergotamine, which is the only thing I know of that could do something like this. Ergotamine is a strong constrictor of blood vessels, and the blood supply to the toes could have been entirely shut off, thus leading to gangrene. He, of course, lost his toes, but otherwise was eventually all right.

On another occasion a man [76-b] was just walking along minding his own business when a sudden pain developed in his eye. This was the history. We took an X-ray and found a bullet lodged at the opening of the optic canal. He had been struck by a stray, nearly-spent bullet. The eye was enucleated and the bullet removed. He will live with one eye, but at least he is alive.

VC COMMANDER

Early one afternoon I got the sense of a general uneasiness from the way some nurses and others out in the courtyard were talking and acting. I was in my office and a man was ushered in for me to see. I sensed that there was something special about him from the way others were treating him. He was concerned about his lingering cough, that it might be TB. I questioned him carefully about it through my interpreter. I was just a little on edge about him. I had my .38 in its holster around my waist as usual. It was hidden from view under the scrub suit, the shirt extending down to cover it. I kept alert and kept my eye on him. I was wary, but didn't want to let him know this. I was careful and respectful in questioning him. One time I saw him glance up at the picture of my wife and children that I had on a shelf on the wall to the side. If he had a weapon and was going to go for it, it was going to be whoever was the quickest on the draw.

After getting the details about his cough, I got up from behind the desk and walked over to him and began listening to his chest with my stethoscope. Just as I thought, when I pulled up his shirt to listen, there was a revolver hidden underneath it. I made a point to pay no particular attention to this as I moved the stethoscope around, listening to his breathing. Then I sent him to Kelly to have an X-ray taken. When this was finished, I showed him the X-ray and explained that it was clear and that I didn't think that he had TB.

I think he may have been assessing my attitude toward him. I had treated him with respect, as though it were irrelevant to me whether he was VC or not. Was he there to do me in on the spot? Was he there to see how I treated my Vietnamese patients? If my actions weren't to his liking, would I be on the VC priority hit list? Or, since I had gotten a reputation for diagnosing TB, was he just a local VC commander concerned that his cough might be TB and had come to me because I was the local expert? The visit ended undramatically. After he left, I sensed a feeling of relief among those outside on the grounds.

CHET ROI (dead already)

One day a CIDG who had been shot in the chest was brought in by helicopter. He was a strapping young man, probably in his early twenties, healthy and strong-looking, cooperative and decent. I remember him sitting there while we were hurriedly removing his shirt to examine him. He didn't look that bad, but he told us, *Chet roi.* I said, *Khum chet* which means not dead. He again said, *Chet roi,* and before we could do anything further, he rapidly worsened and died. The bullet had hit one of the main arteries from the heart.

(As stated before, some of the CIDG were bad eggs and caused trouble, but most of them didn't. Most were courageous like this fellow and were putting their lives on the line.)

3 February

Higgins came in from Ap Bac today for supplies. He's gotten the roof repaired on the dispensary and has the place painted and cleaned up. He still has no interpreter, but should be getting one from Kien Quan II in a few weeks. The VC hit their area three days ago. One friendly was killed and two wounded,

three VC were killed and six wounded. Some mortar fire landed in town and a few rounds came in the small camp where Higgins is staying. When the action started, Higgins grabbed his medic pack, and he and Captain Cantland ran down the road toward the firing. Fields, a conscientious objector who is on our team and was the fourth American in the camp, decided the next day to start carrying a carbine.

We had 13 civilian casualties from an operation Saturday. We worked through the night and through Sunday and didn't finish up with all the cases until Monday.

Tet is nearly here and most of the nurses have left to celebrate it. (This Tet was one year before the ''Tet Offensive'' of historical notoriety.)

9 February

Tet is here: Firecrackers explode everywhere throughout the day. Last night Chuck (Dr. E.), Don Gilhausen and I were invited to celebrate the New Year with Dai uy Fong. He served many kinds of candies, champagne and Chinese wine, which was much too strong to be considered good. At midnight we went outside and lit many firecrackers, as did the townspeople. The machine-gun positions on the edge of town fired tracers into the sky.

Two days ago one of our men came in from Tuyen Nhon. He got drunk and went over the barbed wire at the compound to get downtown at 1 a.m. Dai uy Fong spotted him and tried to get him to come back, but he would not. I think the place is starting to get to him, and we'll have to apply some disciplinary measures.

18 February

I've been told by Dr. Ting that Dai uy Fong's father was murdered in North Vietnam by the Communists. Little wonder he is such an avid anti-Communist. His son is in the U.S. training as a pilot.

Ting also told me that Mr. Song worked in Moc Hoa partly because he had formerly belonged to the Diem party.

I spent the weekend in Saigon. I became quite ill on the airplane to Can Tho. The pilot was kind enough to wait an extra 15 minutes at an intermediary stop. In Can Tho I met with the public health people and discussed the hamlet health worker problem.

Saturday afternoon I arrived in Saigon and met Ting. The trip was intended to obtain more interpreters. Mr. Vuong had recently terminated his work for us and had promised to meet me in Saigon Sunday with several of his friends who might be interested in working as interpreters. He did not show up.

I had dinner with Ting at his father's house. Ting's sister is an English teacher and she will attempt to find an interpreter or two for us in the next few weeks. Ting's sister had studied in the U.S. and a sorority sister of hers, Ingrid Haimans, was also at the house for dinner. She intends to stay in Saigon indefinitely. She is a Swedish girl and has a very important position as one of a three-person team of economic advisors to Vietnam. She told me that 30 percent of the VN budget is supplied directly by U.S. funds. The rest of the funding comes from taxes on imports.

The next night Ting invited me to eat at his father-in-law's home. Among other things, pigs' ears were served.

VC PARTY

During Tet the Chieu Hoi center held a party for VC [75-d]. They advertised this party by leaflet drops. I was in Saigon when it was held, but Eggerstedt went to it. The local security chief was there taking pictures which he intends to enlarge later. There was a large crowd and unbelievably, many of the "prominent" VC of the area attended. One of our old hospital patients was there. He turned out to be a VC district chief of all things. I can hardly believe that such a party could occur, but it did. Apparently, they had various party type games, such as climbing a greased pole and a pig catching contest.

19 February

We've been out of all types of cough syrup at the hospital for two weeks and there is none in the supply depot at Saigon. Things like this keep happening all the time.

A boy died of rabies at our hospital today. This is the first case of rabies I've seen.

22 February

All hell has been breaking loose here the last few days. Today a patrol out of BTT was ambushed and two Special Forces were severely wounded. There were no evacuation choppers to be had immediately and they were without help for two or three hours. Finally a chopper came and landed. Usually they will pick them up and then fly them here temporarily or to Saigon. Anyway, the chopper landed at our hospital first and I jumped in with an emergency kit to go and pick them up. Meanwhile, two evacuation choppers beat us to the pickup and my chopper turned around and headed back to Moc Hoa. About three minutes later the evacuation copters came in.

One of the U.S. people was shot through the back and legs, was coughing up blood and was in shock. The other was shot in the head, chest and abdomen but was conscious and had good blood pressure. The colonel was at the hospital and we got U.S. donors to give blood. We gave one unit of PVP (like plasma) and then started the blood. Then we put them both back on the chopper and McCurley, a Special Forces medic, and I went to Saigon with the wounded. I started another unit of blood while on the way. There was no place to hang the blood bag so we held it up with our hands on the way in. A few miles out of Saigon the Third Field contacted us by radio and asked for a description of the wounds. We were met at the airport by a Third Field Hospital doctor. Mac and I then got back on the copter and returned to Moc Hoa.

When we got back, we found out that a Vietnamese interpreter with them had died shortly after arriving at the hospital and another Vietnamese had lost both of his eyes.

Someone said that today six North Vietnamese Regulars in full uniform walked into Bien Hiep and told the villagers to leave because they were going to overrun the village tonight. There are two U.S. Special Forces and a company of VN in Bien Hiep.

ARRIVAL OF THE DEAD

Now to back up a few days. About three days ago, during the night, a VN CIDG company in Ca Do hamlet (about three miles from here), radioed that they were being overrun. Shortly after, radio contact was lost. Early that morning we received three CIDG who had minor wounds. We were told that there were two

Attack on Ca Do Hamlet.

boatloads of wounded on the way in. It was a clear day and the air was unusually cool. As we waited, all about there was a strange stillness. Even sounds from the town in the distance seemed diminished. Everyone in the hospital seemed frozen in place, awaiting the arrival — of the dead. Two boatloads came in at 10 a.m. There were 16 CIDG and all were dead [76-e]. They appeared to have been shot at close range. They were either shot through the head or heart or abdomen. Many had half their head blown off. Later dead civilians were brought in, probably CIDG family members, dead women and children. The VC had overrun one of the defensive walls of the outpost and the men on the other three walls fled. There were 80 CIDG defending the post.

MORTAR ATTACK

The same evening I was watching a movie at the compound. Suddenly the sergeant major ran in and told us to take our positions, that the USAID house downtown was being mortared. We all ran to our positions in the compound — mine being the medical bunker. I could hear the mortars thudding in. After about ten minutes we received a call from our U.S. people in Sector (VN headquarters) to release the MILPHAP team to the hospital. We scrambled into the jeeps and drove down. As we pulled into the hospital we saw a crowd of 15 to 20 people standing outside, near the entry of the main building. We hurried over and opened the screen doors. I was taken aback by the sight. The wide L-shaped, poorly-lighted hall was completely filled with several hundred people. They were assembled in clusters. The 60-80 wounded were propped or lying at the center of these with other adults and children squatting and milling around them. There was the groaning of the wounded and from those about them emanated a cacophony like a flock of boisterous birds that had just landed in this spot and were all at once voicing their opinions of the circumstances. Yet, strangely, the volume was subdued; there was no loud wailing or screaming. There were waving arms and stumbling nurses. Small children were running hither and yon. Ting and our VPVN surgeon were compressed in a corner attending a patient. Song and some nurses who had arrived shortly before, were helter-skelter applying bandages.

Back in San Antonio we had been instructed how to approach such a mass casualty situation. We needed to assess the injuries quickly, stabilize those in shock and proceed to do debridements on those with less severe injuries, in order to keep this type of injury from converting into a more severe problem. Those cases that would require prolonged surgery, but could be delayed some, were not to be priority. The interpreters were there, fortunately. We had also rehearsed for such an eventuality and so were somewhat prepared.

I positioned myself at the entrance of the medical ward. In the hall in front of me were the multitude of wounded. My men would quickly bring the patients, one at a time from the outpatient area to my position. We tried to scout out the most seriously wounded first. I had stationed some of my men on one side of the medical ward. There they received about 15 seriously wounded, taking blood pressures and starting IV's on those who were in shock.

In the meantime Ting and our VPVN went to the surgical suite and did several cutdowns and shortly started on a splenectomy which was necessary, but which removed them from helping with the other injuries. Vietnamese nurses and some of my men were located near the end of the medical ward. As I sent them the less seriously wounded, they would apply bandages. These were then moved out of the building to the grounds where they were grouped in categories and attended by some of my men and other hospital personnel. Their relatives surrounded them and thus were moved out of the way, out of the hospital and to the grounds. The patients there were rebandaged as necessary, comforted and put on hold until we could start the next step in their care.

All did not go smoothly; some came through more than once, seemingly demanding priority even though their wounds were of a lesser degree than those of others.

After the serious were stabilized, Dr. E. and I started doing debridements in the minor surgery room. For instance, in a case with a piece of mortar through the leg, it is necessary to open the wound and remove the dead and dirty tissue and, if possible, the projectile. If these wounds are not treated in time, they convert into more seriously infected and gangrenous wounds, so time is important. Dr. E. and I, each with an assistant from my team, started on these and worked steadily until daylight, and then continued on until 6 p.m. of that next day. Most of the Vietnamese hospital personnel were present and were quite helpful, especially in resterilizing the instrument trays that had been used so that we could work continuously. Each case took ten to 15 minutes.

After the splenectomy, our VPVN decided to do one of the abdominal cases and so was occupied through most of the night with this. In the a.m. we evacuated ten of the patients — serious abdomen and head injuries. Several of the more serious cases that

73-a Hovercraft.

73-b Hovercraft.

73-c Airboats.

73-d Ap Bac bridge.

73-e Canal out of Ap Bac.

73-f Canal scene.

73-g Grass hut by Nhon Nhin III.

74-a Motoring up small canal to Buc Hoa. From left, front: CIDG trooper, LLDB officer, Higgins, interpreter Kwan behind Higgins.

74-b CIDG children near Kien Quan II.

74-c Clinic at Buc Hoa.

74-d Village children at Buc Hoa.

74-e Sergeant Garcia at Kien Quan II village.

74-f In front of Song's. From left: Boyle, Dr. Eggerstedt, Kelley, Jackson, Song, Song's friend.

74-g Outside at Nguyen's. Third from left: Dr. Harper, McCurley, Nguyen, Jackson, Ting, Eggerstedt.

75-a Helicopters on air strip.

75-b CT platoon.

75-c Song's daughter's wedding.

75-d Below — Games at party for VC.

75-e Top right — Tet charity collection for injured CIDG.

75-f Bottom right — Cornerstone ceremony. From left: minister of health, province chief.

76-a   Hoot-toot-ra-phoot.

76-b   Man with bullet in eye.

76-c   Boy from countryside.

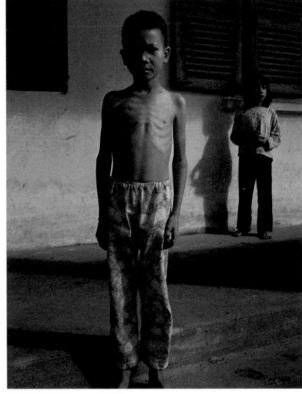

76-d   Orphan with TB.

76-e   Hospital morgue scene after attack on Ca Do hamlet.

76-f   Mine casualty.

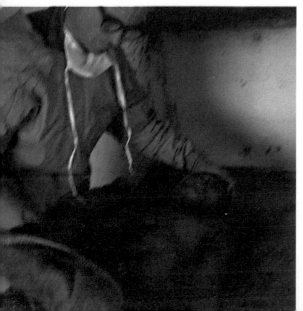

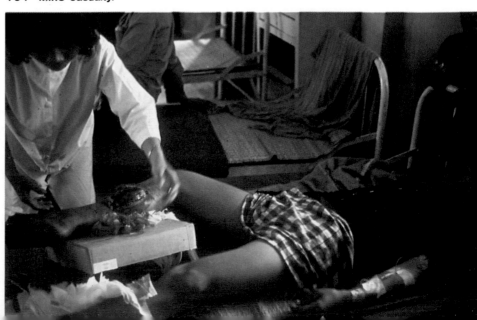

Hospital grounds after mortar attack on town.

we would have time for were kept to be done during the day.

I shall not forget the initial sight and the moaning, commotion and chaos, of the mass of people jammed into the outpatient area. The mortars had landed in the marketplace. Seven persons had been killed immediately and 90 in all had been wounded or killed.

A few months afterward, Higgins, in telling about this, said that there had been an inch of blood on the operating room floor. The bodies had been stacked up like firewood in the supply room and lab, and that this had been enough death and injury to last anyone a lifetime.

22 February continued

The word is that we're supposed to be mortared again tonight. There are supposed to be many VC just across the border in Cambodia.

The VC passed out pamphlets in town a few days ago telling the townspeople to stay away from the Americans because they were going to be hitting our installations between now and March 19.

28 February

Five days ago I flew to Can Tho to attend a meeting at Public Health of the commanders of the Delta MILPHAP teams. The meeting lasted two days and consisted of direction of efforts. Our priority is to be rural health. In the evenings, I had a chance to discuss the present state of affairs of several other teams. I spoke with Lieutenant Commander Jerry Goller of the Navy team at Soc Trang. They had come over with us. The VN medicine chief at their location was very uncooperative. He would not allow them to work in the surgical section of the hospital and would not allow them to treat certain patients on the medical ward as they wished. They were able to work freely only in the medical clinic. Dr. Goller related that he was very tired at present and was just coasting. He said that it would be best if we could just go ahead and colonize the country and let it have its own

government later. Another team was not getting along too well because they were cutting into the private practice of the VN doctors at their location.

The first speaker at the meeting was John Wells, who is in charge of the prosthetic program for the country. Several days later at Tan Son Nhut airport in Saigon I had a chance to talk further to him about the program. He had been in country for a good number of months and has organized a center in Saigon for the construction of artificial limbs. They have just completed the training of a number of Vietnamese who will now be able to make prostheses. Centers are going to be placed in Can Tho, Da Nang, Na Trang and the Military Hospital in Saigon. All will be staffed by these newly-trained prostheses makers. The center in Can Tho is under construction and should be functioning within the month. John feels he has been much too busy and had come over looking for an easier paced life.

2 March

A few months ago Dr. Ting was able to obtain eight million p's ($80,000) from a charitable fund in Saigon to build a new maternity building. He felt he needed only four million and so gave the other half to his medical friend in the province to the south for a hospital project.

Today we were visited by a dozen Saigon dignitaries to lay the cornerstone for this building [75-f]. These were the minister of health, the minister of industry, a female director of a large pharmaceutical firm, the mayor of Saigon, four others from the charitable group and a U.S. colonel advisor. They were to arrive in Moc Hoa first, and then fly to the province to the south (Kien Phong), but they mistakenly reversed the order and our ceremony was delayed several hours. The minister of health informed me that he had information that soon there would be North Vietnamese Regulars in the province and perhaps an attack on Moc Hoa. I told him that I thought the surrounding area was too open for them to risk a large attack, and he then told me that my logic was not good. The group had lunch at the province chief's home and a loud conversation, about what, I know not, was carried on between the minister of health and the mayor of Saigon. The mayor was dressed in a paratrooper's uniform and the minister of health was disheveled as usual, and dressed in a military uniform that didn't fit very well.

Previously, while at Can Tho at a meeting, we were briefed on the present Chieu Hoi program. In 1966 there were 20,000 returnees, at a cost of two million dollars, which is one hundred dollars per returnee. There were 50,000 VC killed or wounded, and the cost is $40,000 per killed VC. The present kill ratio is 3.3 VC per one free world and VN killed.

5 March

On the aircraft on the way to Hong Kong for R&R (rest and recreation) I sat next to a young soldier from the 25th Infantry Division. He is a platoon leader and had been in Vietnam six months. He had spent three months in a hospital in Japan after being wounded in the foot by a mine. He was now back in action. The 25th had been in country since January of '66, 14 months ago. I asked him about casualties.

"A" Company had been the hardest hit. One company consists of about 150 men, and over the year's time, there had been 250 killed in action in this company. From "B" Company — his company — there had been 100 killed in action over the year's time. This seems to be a high toll.

The 25th often works in Tay Ninh Province — a hotspot to the west of Saigon. Booby traps and mines cause most injuries. On one occasion, "B" company had gotten into a minefield; 18 were killed and 8 wounded. He stated that they were often ambushed. I asked what tactics were used to help prevent this. He said that it is difficult to prevent such an ambush. There is a lead man with a trained dog and he is followed by three men, ten yards apart, ahead of the rest. I asked if the dogs were any good, and he said he was not much impressed with them. He stated that live ducks are used to prevent surprise attacks when the patrol is stationary. These are tied on the periphery and are effective.

As an example of an ambush, one day the platoon was ambushed by two VC. One suddenly stood up in front of them and sprayed the lead men with automatic fire. Two GI's were killed and another wounded. The VC escaped.

He told how an outpost of the unit's base camp was overrun a short while ago. The outpost was 400 yards in front of the main camp. It was hit by about 300 VC and apparently all of the 30 GI's had been asleep. All were killed.

8 March

I have been on R&R in Hong Kong for the past five days [93-a]. It's not pleasant thinking of having to go back to Vietnam tomorrow. Hong Kong is a fabulous city — much larger than I expected and in many ways more modern than Milwaukee. The prices are so low that one must buy to take advantage of the opportunity. I purchased things for Bonnie and the relatives. I bought an opal and a few other rings, several wristwatches, a tea set and a number of ivory carvings.

TIGER BAUM GARDENS

One day in Hong Kong I visited the Tiger Baum Gardens. Here there are ornately painted stone figures set along an embankment. Some depict scenes of ancient Chinese battles. One showed the conquerers gleefully torturing in macabre fashion the recently captured inhabitants of a village [93-b]. Some of the villagers were being disemboweled, others beheaded and so forth.

(Such things were soon to be witnessed again on earth. A few years hence in Cambodia atrocities depicted in these scenes would be applied by the Leninist disciple Pol Pot and his followers upon their own defeated people.)

8 March continued

Just a few comments on the Vietnamese people. They are friendly to those of their kind whom they casually know and treat each other with a great deal of courtesy. This courtesy is exemplified by their traffic manners. One rarely sees an exchange of harsh words between two drivers, even though the traffic conditions are exceedingly hectic. In other circumstances where in the U.S. there would often be engendered a caustic exchange of words...in Vietnam this does not take place. Though this courtesy and friendliness exist, they, however, in general, care only for those of their immediate family. Hardly any of them care very much about the welfare of the general public to work at doing something to improve the conditions of the general public. Thus, there are few "dedicated" Vietnamese. Certainly, few in the health field care very much about the general welfare of the people, but then, the people themselves care little. They care only when they are directly affected by illness. They do not heed advice if it requires some discomfort to themselves.

Thus, I have seen many times a child near death brought to the hospital and when, if in the next day he improves, the parents take him and leave, even though they are told that they should stay in order to receive continuing treatment. They leave, I suspect, because it is inconvenient for them to stay. A few will stay. If it is the parents themselves who are ill, they will stay until they are quite well and this is because they can tell that on the second day of hospitalization they are still somewhat ill. So they stay because they recognize they are not yet well, but they will not take the word of the physician in the case of their children that it would be better for them to stay. For a good number of them this is true.

Many of the TB patients who must be treated regularly for one year do not heed the advice for a regular regime of treatment even though they are told that without such treatment they will likely die soon. As soon as they get better, or as it becomes an effort to return to the hospital twice weekly for their medicine, they stop treatment.

(These comments were prompted by my frustration at having patients leave the hospital before completing their treatment. I was upset at the time and really should not have been so harsh in my comments. Most of the Vietnamese I came to know were delightful people. They were more easy going in their ways than was I, for which they should be complimented. I admired this trait in them.)

15 March

Barton and some of the VN nurses have been immunizing at the schools. In the last four days, they've immunized 2,100 school children.

18 March

I was just talking with Lieutenant Cantland in the club this afternoon. Cantland has been the Special Forces person at Ap Bac where Higgins is and has been there for three months. He has been ordered to report back to the States immediately for discharge. He had previously applied for extension of his duties in the Army and in Vietnam, but although he had received word that he would be able to stay in the Army, those papers had been lost and now suddenly he must report back to the States. He had many complaints of the support the people were given in his area by the VN government. Pigs for breeding had been promised to the people. The government avoided the program because it was decided that it would be too expensive. Other things have been promised, none of which have come about. In fact, according to him, the only thing we've done for the people of the area is not bomb their villages.

Vuong and Binh, my two best interpreters, came to me this morning and told me that they had been terrorized again by the VN [93-c]. This was not the first incident. I felt that their lives were in danger and decided to have them flown to Can Tho for reassignment. That leaves me with two interpreters. I had made a report of this which is described below.

Two MILPHAP interpreters, Mr. Vuong and Mr. Binh, have been threatened on a number of occasions by various local Vietnamese troops. The following is a description of these threats.

The first incident occurred four months ago. The interpreters were visiting a male English school teacher friend and were conversing in English. Purportedly a member of the local CT platoon overheard this conversation and informed them that he did not like conversations in English. Later that evening four members of the CT platoon pointed rifles at the two interpreters and told them to move out of that house. This incident was not brought to my attention until several months later and even then, the interpreters were reticent about the matter.

On another occasion Mr. Binh was in the market and happened to be wearing sunglasses. Purportedly a CIDG told him to take these off or he would shoot him.

A third incident occurred when we were downtown and using the interpreters to help us buy things in the local market. The next day the interpreters were told by the CIDG to stay away from the Americans and stop being so friendly with them.

Another incident occurred during the recent mass casualty situation. Purportedly a CIDG or relative of a CIDG was injured and was told that his injury was not serious and that he would be further treated several hours later after we had attended some others. The interpreter was threatened in this instance by the CIDG. The interpreters did not bring this to my attention.

A few days ago the interpreters were at a shop and noticed that a CIDG across the street was watching them. They left the shop and afterward were told that shortly thereafter, five CIDG came into the shop asking where they were.

On another occasion a few days ago while they were in a restaurant, a number of CIDG got behind and in front of them and threatened them. The interpreters became frightened and ran from the restaurant. The interpreters told me about this incident and I reported this to the U.S. commander of the A-Team in Moc Hoa, and he informed me that he would relate this to his counterpart to inform his troops to cease harassment of the interpreters.

One day ago the interpreters were in a restaurant. Supposedly, a Captain Trung Son of the LLDB was seated at an adjacent table with several CIDG. He got up, with rifle over shoulder and walked around the interpreters' table and stated that if anyone gave his CIDG any trouble, they would be torn apart. (I suspect this probably was not Son, but someone impersonating him.)

That evening two CIDG with grenades in their hands were noticed walking about the outside of the interpreters' apartment. The landlord, a RF (Regional Force) soldier, told the interpreters that if the CIDG entered the house, he would throw a grenade at the CIDG. The next morning the interpreters informed me about this incident and the incident concerning Captain Son. It was decided that Moc Hoa was no longer safe for them and they were sent to Can Tho for reassignment. They have given me a partial name of a CIDG who had threatened them in the past. He is called Hai and purportedly is just out of jail. He was a deserter and had organized "hold-ups" in the past. They call him, "The most terrible man in Moc Hoa."

The interpreters do not know why they have been threatened. I can only make a guess at the reason. Perhaps the CIDG wish preferential treatment at our hospital and are attempting to get this by terrorizing our interpreters such that, for example, they will be seen first in line at the outpatient department. This may be entirely wrong and it may be simply general irresponsibility and lack of discipline in the CIDG that has brought this about. My interpreters have told me that they by no means are the only people in town who are terrorized by the CIDG.

We hope action will be taken locally so that the remaining two interpreters will not be threatened.

(I wonder if some of these problem CIDG may have been VC trying to disrupt things. I was not especially afraid of the CIDG or bothered by them otherwise. I treated them nicely enough in the hospital and we treated many of them for battle wounds and for outpatient illnesses. It was a small minority that were troublemakers.)

19 March

There was an air strike to the south of us this morning and this afternoon we received nine casualties. One died in the operating room. Another from elsewhere had his right foot blown off by a mine [76-f].

24 March

One of the longest operations since we've been here occurred on 20 March and lasted three days [93-e]. We received a steady stream of casualties, most from booby traps. Several CIDG were shot as they were getting on a helicopter.

Today Dr. Marsh and Lew Smith and a VPVN from Can Tho — Dr . Welsh arrived. Dr. Welsh came to consult with Dr. Eggerstedt on several patients. Marsh and Smith were here to give me support with the interpreter situation. All week I had been steaming mad about the loss of my interpreters. I had requested that Colonel F. arrange a meeting with himself, the LLDB commander and me so that I could convey to them that this was no little thing that had occurred and could not pass lightly. I wanted them to know how distraught I was and how important it was to our functioning that we have an adequate number of interpreters.

Yesterday, Colonel F. and I were supposed to have met with Dai uy Son. When we arrived we were told that Son had left and was having breakfast in the market, so the meeting was scheduled for 9 a.m. today. This morning I was told that it would be at 10 a.m. rather than nine. Dr. Marsh and Lew Smith arrived at 8:30 and we went to USAID and spoke with the acting province representative about the situation. Al Nacke, the police counterpart, is acting in this capacity during the absence of Art Elmore.

Mr. Nacke related that this was not the only incident of significance attributed to the CIDG. He mentioned the case of murder and rape by a CIDG, and that the camp commander would not release the guilty individual to the police. He also told about the CIDG stopping river traffic at Me Phu Tay to collect tax — just like the VC — and thus cutting the river traffic off to Moc Hoa. After this discussion it was time for the meeting with Dai uy Son in Colonel F.'s office at the B-Team. Marsh and Smith attended this meeting. The colonel presented the aforementioned report to Dai uy Son.

Son denied he was personally involved. Dai uy Son is rather tall for a Vietnamese and seemed intelligent and a bit philosophical at times. He mentioned that he had many troops and that they were difficult to control at times. He stated that we must be careful to identify just who the soldiers involved are, for there are RF, PF and CT platoon soldiers, and not just CIDG in Moc Hoa. He said that the interpreters were not necessarily wholly innocent, and one had said that the CIDG must respect the interpreters, because without doctors there would be no help for the CIDG. I was impressed by Son and it seemed to me that it would have been out of character for him to have been the person that the interpreters encountered in the restaurant. I suspected one of the CIDG had likely impersonated Son there. Nevertheless, this discussion would at least let him know how bothered we were about losing these interpreters.

The colonel seemed much more concerned about my manner of presenting the incidents than the incidents themselves. He was critical that the report was presented to appear to be all fact and that I had not brought up the incidents as they had occurred. Dr. Marsh and Lew Smith were quite unhappy with the colonel's seeming lack of interest in the matter. Dr. Marsh believes that the only way to prevent future incidents is to go to the top and have these people provide a mechanism for better discipline of the CIDG. The LLDB are actually afraid to discipline the CIDG. Perhaps they fear that if they did impose strict discipline, they might be shot by the CIDG on the battlefield. Marsh will probably talk to General Humphries about the matter.

Ong Song will be out of town for two weeks. I now have to do the anesthesia. This is the first time I've ever given anesthesia and it's quite interesting. I've had two cases so far. I use pentothal for induction and then give ether with our ether anesthesia machine. No trouble so far.

5 April

Today six CIDG casualties from Tuyen Nhon came in. Three had severe hand injuries. They must have been holding an explosive — not a grenade.

Three days ago a new interpreter came, but left the next day after hearing what had occurred with the other interpreters.

(I remembered how upset I was on losing the interpreters. Things worked so much better when enough of them were around. It put a real crimp on things when three doctors had to share one interpreter.)

Dr. Ting received the OK from the Ministry of Health to start a three-month course at our hospital for 20 hamlet health workers. (Several months ago I had pushed to get such a course started, but was told that we first needed the approval of the Ministry of Health.) We'll take about half of those previously trained by the Special Forces course and run them through this course so that they can be paid by the Ministry of Health.

It had come to my attention that the latrine at the hospital was blocked up. Patients were going to open areas just outside of the hospital grounds to defecate. Some weeks ago I had talked to Barton, who is the most practical man on our team, to see if he could find some way to fix this. After some time he was able to obtain a pump and hoses, and yesterday was able to pump out the septic tank. None of the Vietnamese health workers would help him. They knew when to keep their distance.

8 April

To mention the pace of the casualties, on the sixth we received four casualties. Yesterday we received two and today a young boy was brought in too late.

We're making a small lecture room out of my office. We've built a decent blackboard and are having the prisoners construct some benches for the 20 expected pupils. In turn, we'll give the prisoners rice, wheat, soap and a small amount of money.

I am going to start to push quite hard to get some cleanliness about the place. The girl at the outpatient department desk was in the habit of throwing various pieces of paper on the floor about her desk rather than in the wastebasket ten feet away. She was quite surprised when I told her that I would expect her to stop this and use the wastebasket. At the medical ward stations, paper bits and bandages were strewn on the floor. I told six health workers at the station that they must pick these up and not wait for the laborers to clean up. Two got up, but instead of helping pick up, pretended to have something else to do. Several did help clean up. The two laborers on the medical ward side continue to hide and try to get out of work every chance they get, and I'm not about to stand for it much longer. Before, on complaining to Ting about this, he stated that the pay is very low and no one else could be hired to do the work, but this is foolishness.

Today Sergeant Barton had them picking up paper on the grounds. One left and when Barton asked the other about this, he said that he went home for breakfast. Well, I won't stand for this business and either Ting straightens them out or we'll find some way to pressure him into it.

Some of these people are abysmally lazy and this, at times, includes everyone from Dr. Ting to the nurses on down, especially the nurses. Right now I can think of only three people at the hospital who could not ever be called lazy — Mr. Song, Nguyen and Mr. Ngok, the medical ward nurse.

(Obviously I lost my temper and overstated things a bit.)

Yesterday I told the girl at the outpatient desk to wash the outpatient thermometer at 4 p.m. and put alcohol in the container, and then in the morning, to pour out this alcohol and return the thermometer to the outpatient desk. If this gets done, I'll be very surprised. I know I'll have to prod her daily for a while and then check intermittently on her later — such laziness.

(On reflection about this I wonder if rather than laziness, it was more them not wanting to have me tell them what to do in what were perceived as minor matters. Perhaps they thought I was taking over Ting's area of authority and they were going to be passively resistant and show me that I couldn't boss them around. For all I know, Ting may have told them to act this way for a while. For some time I was getting few results with them. I finally went and talked to Ting about it, and then they improved. If someone was injured or sick, they would follow my instructions to help energetically and willingly, but this kind of janitoring apparently was not to be my business. I was overstepping my authority. They weren't going to let the American doctor tell them where or where not to throw the garbage.)

Outside Tuyen Nhon clinic.

Inside clinic at Tuyen Nhon.

12 April

In Tuyen Nhon a hamlet policeman was assassinated recently and now none of the eight hamlet health workers from that area want to go out into the respective hamlets as we had hoped they would. We'll just have to keep them at the district dispensary and have the rest go out as before on medical patrols.

They're shooting up quite a few flares tonight just south of the hospital and I heard one burst of gunfire.

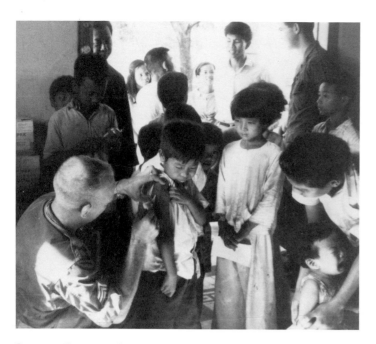

Sergeant Barton and nurse immunizing.

At Ap Bac clinic. McCurley, VN health worker, Fields.

17 April

NIGHT FOR FROGS

Two days ago a man was admitted during the night. A call came to the B-Team on the radio to tell us to come to the hospital, and so we got up and drove down in the jeeps. It had recently rained, and it was dark, wet, warm and muddy. As I stepped from the jeep my boots slid in the muck. It was a good night for frogs. Several of the nurses met us outside on the porch and we stood there awhile as they described why they had called us. The patient was vomiting and we were told that he had swallowed a frog. We looked at them questioningly, in mild disbelief, and then we were told that frogs are poisonous and maybe he wanted to commit suicide. So in we went to see him. Well, when I listened to his heart, the rate was slowed way down to 38 per minute and I thought he must have a heart block. We had no good medicine for this, but tried what we had which was not as strong as we would have preferred. By the next morning his heart rate was back to normal. I think it was something in the frog skin that did this to him. What a strange way to commit suicide. At least this time it didn't work.

17 April continued

Three days ago I sent out two of the new hamlet health workers (12 had been trained) [93-f, h] to Ap Bac with Fields. Higgins had left for one month leave in the States. We had sent Higgins into Can Tho to pay a bill and pick up paint. He was given $40 to buy paint. Rylant sent him there and told him that if he didn't have enough to pay his debt he should go to Saigon to draw advanced pay. While there he stopped at the MACV surgeons office and was told that his leave was imminent and not to return to Moc Hoa. He had extended and will be back here for six months after leave. Anyway, we don't have our paint and his bill is unpaid.

I had to put someone with more experience than Fields in Ap Bac and told McCurley to move there from Kien Quan. McCurley showed up the next day and put in a 1049, which is a request to transfer out of the unit. I approved it with the reservation that he not be allowed to leave until an adequate replacement arrives. McCurley decided to stay.

Two days ago I sent another health worker to Bac Hoa, which is a Catholic hamlet of 2,000 just north of Kien Quan. She lives there, and so that should work out well. I have another one from there who will take the next course at our hospital.

We are trying to have all those hamlet workers who were trained by the Special Forces trained at our new course [93-g]. Half will be trained the next three months and the other half, six months later. This is so that their pay can come from the Ministry of Health channels rather than Special Forces.

Within the next few days I'll send out two more to Bac Chan, a hamlet several clicks (kilometers) to the northwest of here up the Vam Co Tay River.

Tomorrow I'm sending one with Williams to Kien Quan. She seems a bit apprehensive. Kien Quan is not one of the better places to live.

21 April

Two days ago a force from Kien Quan went into the Pocket area without air support. They were hit hard and a Special Forces sergeant who had been here at the B-Team in Moc Hoa was killed [94-a]. A mortar exploded just behind him and blew him ten feet forward. A sergeant who was just in front of him told me about this, and the blast had also knocked him off his feet, but he was uninjured. About ten CIDG were killed and the hospital received six or seven casualties that morning [94-b]. A large reaction force was brought in, but could not penetrate into the area where some CIDG were still trapped. Helicopters could not get in to evacuate the wounded. They finally were able to get them out by dark, but had to carry their 20 or so casualties back to Kien Quan, and the trip took the entire night.

Today they had a large, seven-company operation in division area. There was negative contact, but VC mines killed three CIDG and wounded seven. The operation at noon switched to the Pocket to extract three bodies they had had to leave behind two days before. Contact was made, but was brief. Fifty VC were spotted and an air strike was called into the area.

Another hamlet health worker left for work today. She went to Bac Chan which is a half-hour ride by bicycle. I suppose she'll commute every day, at least I hope she'll commute safely.

They now have the road open to Ap Bac. A small convoy is going tomorrow.

I was just talking with Bird-Dog (spotter plane pilot), who got three VC today with his rockets down in the Pocket. The ground troops also got three VC. He says that the ground troops walked by a lot of VC. The VC hide in ''spider holes'' — small areas which are covered and hard to spot, but he said that the ground troops don't want to find them either and so just walk by if they do see one.

Chuck was again teaching the midwives English. They were discussing celebrations. The VN celebrate deaths and thought it very humorous that we celebrate birthdays, especially with birthday cakes.

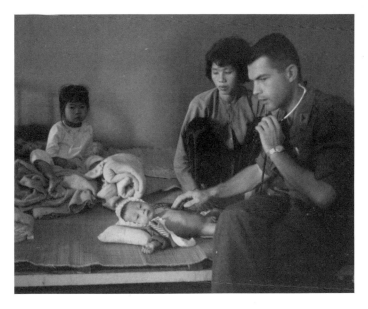

Dr. Eggerstedt checking infant.

D. E. was telling me how, in working for military intelligence in Saigon, he was called to treat a former VC lieutenant colonel who had come in as a Chieu Hoi. The colonel had an attack of falciparum malaria and was very ill. Dr. E. was not able to get him admitted to a hospital for U.S. servicemen. He was not allowed by the VN to see the patient a second time. The U.S. advisor, who had called Dr. E. in on the case, had been told by his VN counterpart that he was acting just like the French in acting on his own to call in an American doctor. Hopefully, he was treated through the VN medical system. The colonel, prior to his illness, had been cooperative and had given much valuable information. He had been stationed in the "Iron Triangle." Here was a chance to keep his cooperativeness and this was likely blown by the VN by their not allowing Dr. E. to care for the patient.

22 April

There has been a report that the VC are gaining prestige in parts of the province by paying the peasants for pigs that are stolen by the CIDG on operations.

Sixty have been caught drawing double pay by being registered as both CIDG and RF troops, and an LLDB is getting a rake-off on this. PF troops are paid 1,200 p/month, RF get 24,000 p/month and CIDG get 2,800 p/month.

26 April

Yesterday, we received a Chieu Hoi with a grenade injury to the abdomen. He had eight holes in his intestine, but I think we fixed him up OK. Today we received a CIDG who was shot by one of our helicopters by mistake. The bullet made six holes in his gut and tore his bladder apart. He's going to have a rough time of it. Then, we got two boys about ten years of age who were wounded by a grenade while fishing (likely they were using the grenade to stun the fish). One was wounded in the abdomen, again with eight holes in his gut. Later, Dr. Holswade, our VPVN who had just recently arrived, said that the injuries were the result of a VC booby trap they had blundered into; a third boy had been killed.

28 April

Four M.D. members of the "Committee of Responsibility," a pacifist group headed by Dr. Spock (Spock was not along) came to Moc Hoa. I'll tell about

their visit a bit later. Lieutenant Karo said that I should have told him that they were pacifists. I told him that these people were for capitulation and wanted to see a Communist victory. He said that when he gets back, if any pacifist gives him any trouble, he will flatten him. He then told how he knocked someone off a bar stool who had insulted the Special Forces. This took place in 1963 when the Special Forces were still a small, highly-trained group. He hit him in the mouth, and he fell forward over the bar, then he hit him again and knocked him off the bar stool, and his head hit the floor hard.

CAI CAI — KIM BOOIE AMBUSH

Lieutenant K. went on to describe his first battle experience in Cai Cai (a Special Forces camp in Kien Phong). They had an intelligence report that some VC were going to go into Kim Booie for supplies and so Lieutenant K. and a platoon of CIDG went out at night to set up a morning ambush along the river leading to town. He and an interpreter were located forward from the rest of the platoon. At 9 a.m. he heard laughter of many voices up the river. The first sampan appeared with a single man standing up and looking about — the scout. Lieutenant K. kept hidden behind the ridge along the bank. The second boat contained three men with weapons. Lieutenant K. let them approach and when they were parallel to the bank, one of them spotted him, and Karo opened up on them with automatic fire from his M-16 and got all three. All hell broke loose and rounds were hitting and kicking dirt into his face. Suddenly his interpreter fell on his shoulder — shot through the head. Lieutenant K. put a second clip in and sprayed the area, and now the CIDG squad got into action. Another VC boat was hit and one VC was shot in the head trying to swim to the opposite bank. Two CIDG stood up in the fire fight without regard for all the bullets flying around. One swung the butt of a carbine at a VC trying to flee and fractured his skull. Lieutenant K. ran to where he had left his radio and called the base camp, but could not make contact. He then called May Day, May Day (he did not realize that was the distress call for a downed aircraft). He made contact with a helicopter and two Mohawks which joined the fight within five minutes. When all was over, 17 VC had been killed. The third VC sampan had had a Browning Automatic Rifle mounted on the front and was the gun that was kicking up the dirt in front of Lieutenant K. and that had shot his interpreter in the head.

Cai Cai — Kim Booie Ambush.

Lieutenant Karo on another occasion had made the headlines in the States. His camp was located one mile from Cambodia, and a 70-man Cambodian outpost was located just across the border. One night the VC set up a mortar 150 yards from the Cambodian outpost and began walking mortar shells toward the A-Camp. The VC mortar was spotted from the observation tower and Karo ordered return fire. The first rounds of the return fire blew apart a corner wall of the Cambodian outpost and killed seven Cambodians. Subsequent fire got the VC mortar position.

COMMITTEE OF IRRESPONSIBILITY

Back to the pacifist group, though to call them that, in my mind, is a misnomer. They have been making a tour of medical facilities throughout Vietnam. They explained that their mission was misunderstood and that they were here to find out how many children had received injuries that could not be handled in Vietnam and were looking into possibilities of sending those to hospitals in the States. This is fine, though I would much rather see some other group set up such a program. However, likely their more main purpose was to gain anti-war propaganda.

(From their later reports it was evident that they were looking for civilian casualties, particularly dramatic ones if they could find them that could be used for their purposes. They were not interested in casualties caused by the VC which were in abundance to be seen; these would not serve their purpose.)

We first took them to Dr. Ting's office and presented them with our statistics on casualties. They had a missionary interpreter and had two microphones for continuous recording. We related that there were few such injured that we could think of that would benefit from hospitalization in the States. Mr. Song brought in posters describing the mining of a bus last year and the atrocities of an attack by the VC on a Catholic hamlet where the priest was beheaded. Lieutenant Rylant's casualty figures did not jive with Dr. Ting's, and they were quite interested as to why. As it turned out, Dr. Ting did not enumerate evacuees. We then took them about the wards where we had ten civilians wounded by VC mines or booby traps, three Chieu Hoi wounded by VC mines, one VC, one VC suspect, one CIDG shot accidentally by a U.S. helicopter, one woman shot by a U.S. plane and a patient with a minor burn who had picked up

an unspent rocket. They took many pictures and left their recorders running. We had a patient who had, according to the story, put a grenade in a fire and this mutilated his face, blinded him in both eyes and blew both his hands off. I mentioned that this was an unlikely story and that he probably was planting it when it went off.

We then went to the B-Team for lunch. I asked them what was Dr. Spock's position on how to end the war. They tried to refer the question to the missionary, implying at the same time that they would rather not talk about the subject, but I pressed the issue. They stated that no one knew for certain, but believed that he was anti-war and just what further they did not know. I asked if the Committee of Responsibility had a common opinion. They stated only that it was against the war, and on further details most members differed. I asked the man at my right for his personal opinion. He said that he thought that some form of coalition government would have to be forthcoming. I then asked if he thought that this wouldn't mean a Communist takeover. I stated that I would like to see an end to the war too, but not by Communist takeover. The man to my left said that all would have been settled in 1954 had the South allowed elections. I said that the North had 17 million people and the South 15 million and that with rigged and untruthful propagandized elections, of course, the northern Communists would take over. I stated that given proper knowledge about the true consequences of this, they would not so vote. I said that yes, I was against Communism and was against any election without the people being given fair and proper knowledge of the subsequent consequences, particularly voting themselves out of ever being able to vote again in the future. For voting in Communism will mean voting away the chance to determine their governing bodies in the future and given knowledge of this, they would not vote away this freedom.

(I recall what was said on 18 December. The VC were very effective in putting forth their propaganda, especially to the uneducated, convincing them of the untruth that the U.S. intentions in the war were to colonize the country as the French had done.)

The missionary was talking to Dr. Holswade (VPVN) and stated that he thought that the atrocities were equal on both sides. I told him that from what I know, 90 percent of the casualties to civilians in our hospital are caused by the VC. The man to my left, the most belligerently radical, said, "What about the B-52's?" I said that I did not know what casualties they caused because there had been no B-52 raids in our province since my arrival. I said that in our province there were several VC controlled areas where bombing was done by fighters and that the people had the option of moving out into safe resettlement areas or becoming Chieu Hoi. (An hour later they were to be taken on a tour to the resettlement areas.) He vehemently stated that he thought this was too much to "expect" of peasants who had lived all their lives in one area. The discussion went to the casualties that were being caused by the VC mines. The man on the left stated that with what other weapons would I expect the VC to fight. I told him that I didn't "expect" them to be fighting at all. They shouldn't be trying to take over by fighting in the first place.

A PROCESS OF EVIL

It was well known that the majority of the peasants did not wish to be fighting. They would have been most pleased to have been left alone. Most significantly, there would have been no fighting without the actions of the minority VC. The ultimate initiators of the aggression were the Communist North Vietnamese disciples of Leninist revolutionary doctrine. These perpetrators of violent overthrow, most particularly the leaders, bear the blame for the resultant casualties, including civilian. Foisting Communism down the throats of an otherwise peaceable people through violence is an act of brutality, despicable and heinous. For this to be perceived as glorious revolution is incomprehensible. **Leninist ideation of violent revolutionary overthrow** resulting in death and destruction to thousands **is — a Process of Evil**.

IN DEFENSE OF DEFENSE

It was abundantly clear to most of us (U.S. and South Vietnamese troops) that **we were defenders against** the perpetration of **this Process of Evil**.

28 April continued

The discussion ended when it became time to start the convoy to Ap Bac. Several posters had been placed for them to see [94-h]. At the hospital was a sign stating that peace will come when there is no more Communism. Another said the NLF (National Liberation Front) is nothing but murderers and saboteurs and another at the airport said that the peo-

ple of Kien Tuong strongly resent attempts to appease the Communists by the Unresponsible Committee.

Lieutenant Rylant, Nguyen and I rode in one jeep. The colonel and sergeant major in another, USAID's Jeff Harris and two of the committee in another and several trucks of troopers comprised the convoy. We rode over three bridges that had been blown previously [94-c, d, e]. The first half of the trip to Tan Lap was quite picturesque [94-f, g]. The second half of the trip was rather bleak country — Plain of Reeds. We arrived at Ap Bac where there were more posters and the local amputees had been gathered at the dispensary by Mr. Lonn whom Dr. Ting had sent ahead. I spoke about our rural health program, and then we took two boats four kilometers down the canal to the Chieu Hoi village which is under construction [94-i]. On the way back I was taking some pictures (I had my carbine slung over my shoulder). One picture was taken of some children swimming. I turned around and quickly got the picture. One of the committee asked if I was as good a shot with the carbine as with the camera. I said I was not very good, but had shot a few ducks. He asked what kind of ducks — incredibly seeming to ask if I had meant people. I replied that during the wet season the ducks lose their cover and are easier to find, and that there are also some large crane-like birds that we shoot. As we rode past a home, there was a domestic duck outside, and he asked if I thought that was fair game. I said certainly not. How asinine these people are to imply that I might be out shooting people. I'd shoot the carbine in defense, but not otherwise.

That Cao-Dai. According to my interpreter — "Here is the place VC often appear to catch boats and people and sometimes kill the people."

We returned to Moc Hoa and the trip was again very picturesque. The committee followed Lieutenant Rylant and me, who were riding with Jeff Harris and Dr. Ting. We returned to Moc Hoa, finding the aircraft for their return on the field. The missionary interpreter wished us well and to continue our efforts. One of the four who had earlier said that since coming over, he was able to see some of the falsehood in certain anti-war propaganda back home, shook my hand vigorously. The other three departed without a word.

Our latest volunteer surgeon, Dr. Holswade, had been on this excursion to Ap Bac. When he returned to the States, he wrote a report about his experiences and sent me this information in a letter. On arrival he was struck by the rubbish, barbed wire and sandbags in Saigon. In a briefing he was told that Moc Hoa was one of several Catholic refugee centers. Twelve years ago those fleeing from the North were resettled in these places. He was also told that the VC in Moc Hoa were well organized and would quickly know his attitudes and personal habits, such as if he walked or rode to the hospital. On arrival in Moc Hoa he was immediately bothered by the adverse sanitation at the hospital compared to that of a U.S. hospital. (We strove to improve conditions, but it was a constant problem because of the attitudes and habits of the people. Were we to turn the Vietnamese into the Dutch? They didn't want this.) He was amazed how the families would accompany the injured person to the hospital. They would give the patient added nursing care, prepare his food — cooked on a small fire in the hospital yard — and minister to his every need — except donate blood to him, which they were very reluctant to do.

One time he had refused to admit to the hospital a CIDG who had a minor infection of his face. A couple of nights later a .45 slug went through the screen of his quarters, striking two feet from his head. After that he liberalized his admission policy. He told of the "Committee of Responsibility," looking for children with burns and that they had found so few that some thought they were being concealed from them. He mentioned that in the U.S. press, not much is said about civilians wounded by the VC, that instead there is a constant focus on civilians injured through American action. Of the casualties he saw, half were civilian and half Vietnamese troops. The bulk of the wounds had been inflicted by the Viet Cong, either by gunfire, mortar, grenade, booby traps or land mines. Wounds of lower extremities requiring amputation were quite often seen in peasants, women and children who had touched off booby traps set by the VC. He told how his attitude toward the war had changed since coming here. He and the other

eight doctors that had come over with him had all ended up closer to being hawks than doves. He felt that we must strive to win the hearts and minds of the peasants and intensely wage the rural pacification program.

29 April

From Lieutenant Karo I learned that a Chieu Hoi company had been organized and they had been running counter-terrorist missions into their former territory and were very successful.

2 May

Five more casualties again today — only one serious though. These were from the A-Camp under B-41 in Me Phu Tay in Kien Phong Province.

The hamlet health worker from Bac Hoa came in today. She had been placed there the middle of last month at the clinic, which had had only a midwife. She brought in a patient record book with neatly written record of name and type of treatment and illness. I was very impressed and very happy that she is doing so well. She has seen 110 patients over the past two weeks.

3 May

Two more casualties today; they came from the new A-Camp at Me An in Kien Phong. One was hit above the sternum by a bullet. I put in a chest tube and a lot of blood came out. The other had a bullet enter just above his right buttock and a large amount of blood was accumulating in his left lower chest wall, so the bullet must have hit some intestinal structures. His blood pressure was zero when I first saw him. We got his blood pressure up with plasma expanders and blood and stabilized him.

A woman with Beri-Beri also came in from Me An today. Me An is in VC territory in Kien Phong.

The U.S. Ninth Division is operating south and east of A-415 in our province. This is the first time a U.S. infantry unit has operated in our province.

7 May

I asked Dr. Ting where Dai uy Fong has been. He said he had been in Saigon and was thinking of going there because of difficulties here. A certain group, supposedly including the province chief, has stored in a warehouse a portion of commodities that should have been given away as flood relief and is intending to sell them. Dai uy Fong has been investigating this and if it involves the province chief, of course, he'll have trouble.

Captain Cates, the L-19 Bird Dog pilot, was transferred out recently. In the last three months his aircraft had taken 19 hits. Last month he had 25 VC kills. The total VC killed in the province for that month had been 69. He had taken a lot of chances to draw fire and then returned the fire with rockets on the L-19. I guess they transferred him because they figured he had taken his share of chances.

ITCHYNOSE

One fine afternoon I was sitting in my office minding my own business, when I heard a commotion outside. I looked out the door and nearby on the grounds some of the nurses and Ong Song seemed to be encouraging a young woman to go up the steps to my office. She seemed a bit reluctant. She was dressed to kill with her decorated umbrella and *ao dai* (Vietnamese lady's dress with side slits) and lots of makeup — not the type of female patient I usually saw. I ducked back in and waited to see what would happen. They seemed to present her to me as a patient. I told my interpreter to ask what was her problem. The translation came back that ''her nose itches.'' So, I looked at the side of her nose where she pointed and could see nothing, and told the interpreter to tell her so. She seemed upset at this reply and said something back which translated was that her nose itches and I should look again. I thought that sometimes leprosy could do such a thing and so looked closely again, but still could see nothing and told her so. On translation she seemed even more upset,

and the visit ended in what seemed to be confusion on both sides.

On reflecting about this I think maybe Song was trying to find a way to get me to stay in Vietnam and thought that if I had a Vietnamese wife, I would be more likely to do so, and so he went about finding a local candidate for me. This wasn't too hard to do because men were in short supply. I think the nose bit may have been a type of ''come-on,'' and I was just too dumb to catch on at the time. Anyway, I wouldn't have gone along with this had I caught on, so it was probably better that it ended the way it did.

16 May

Last week I went to Can Tho on business concerning several referral patients and to arrange leave for Bangkok. Jackson and I drove out to Binh Tuy, a large airbase about three miles out of Can Tho. Jackson got some lab equipment from the dispensary there. The night before, they had received 80 rounds of 81mm mortar fire. The VC had overrun a bunker outside the camp and set up their mortar in the bunker.

I had recently hired one of the VN girls from the club to work as an interpreter for the hospital. She was not good, but could do OK.

A new VPVN, Dr. Carl Ruppert has arrived and he has been quite busy. On his first day here we received 26 battle casualties. More than half we had to evacuate to Can Tho to share the workload.

TUYEN NHON

I spent the past weekend in Tuyen Nhon [95-a, b]. I took Fields with me to get the cementing of the dispensary floor started. USAID sent the cement down several weeks ago, but when I got there I found that the delay was that the district wanted to sell the necessary sand and the Special Forces captain in charge felt they should provide it free since it was their dispensary. Anyway, he agreed to purchase it so Fields could start. Fields began the second day we were there. I also had the VN dispensary worker start an inventory of the drugs that had been locked up since the death of the dispensary chief and had him make those available for use.

Fields is also to construct shelves and a cabinet for the midwife. The dispensary [95-c] had been functioning quite well. Brown had had new screens put on. I'll return Friday to see what progress has been made [95-d, f, g].

The second day they talked me into going up the river on a medical patrol [95-e]. We went quite a distance to a place where thirty huts were being finished. These people had been relocated recently from VC territory. We set up in one of the huts. The people were quite friendly. I talked to them about nutrition and sanitation and treated a few for ear infestations and skin disease. All of a sudden there was a lot of rapid shooting from across the river where our CIDG guards had been left. I thought for a moment that this might be an attack and we got a bit edgy. Then there was another outburst of fire. From the pattern of the shooting I suspected that more likely the CIDG guard was trying to have a little fun and make us think that there was an attack starting to see if they could get us to come running out of the hut. We stayed where we were and I suppose spoiled their entertainment.

On medical patrol out of Tuyen Nhon.

92

93-a   Hong Kong.

93-b   Tiger Baum Gardens in Hong Kong.

93-c   From left: interpreter, Barton, interpreter, Eggerstedt, me.

93-d   Me at office lecture room.

93-e   Airfield with Hueys.

93-f   Lecturing hamlet health worker students.

93-g   Hamlet health worker students.

93-h   Students.

94-a   Memorial dedication for killed Special Forces from our area.

94-b   Helicopter bringing dead CIDG. Mother and son await last arrival of father.

94-c   Blown bridge just outside of Moc Hoa.

94-d   Lookout tower at edge of Moc Hoa.

94-e   On road to Ap Bac.

94-f   Fisherman.

94-g   Fisherman by day.

94-h   Myself and Rylant.

94-i   At Chieu Hoi village.

95-a   A-Camp at Tuyen Nhon.

95-b   Road from Tuyen Nhon A-Camp toward clinic.

95-c   Clinic at Tuyen Nhon ghosttown. There was reported to be a minefield in back of the clinic. We stayed in the front.

95-d   Ghost village by clinic. This had been partially built up, but had been overrun and destroyed by the VC.

95-e   Cargo boat on canal. What could have been hidden beneath its cargo?

95-g   On clinic road out of Tuyen Nhon.

95-f   Building thatched hut on road to clinic.

96-a   Bangkok temple.

96-b   Golden Buddha.

96-c   Choppers
at hospital gate.

96-d   Moc Hoa sunset.

Seeing patients in a thatched hut.

19 May

It was very busy again in the outpatient department this a.m. I saw about 100 people. The VN health worker who works there took off without letting me know about it and won't be back for a week. So did the VN who substitutes for him when he is gone. I had been trying to get them to examine patients, not just sit behind a desk and listen to the complaint and write out a day's worth of medicine. So they've pulled a fast one and left me to take care of everyone. I let Mr. Song know we weren't here so they could holiday, but were here to work side-by-side.

This afternoon I managed to get a USAID helicopter and spent an hour in Tuyen Nhon. Fields had done a fine job in finishing the cementing of the floor in the dispensary there.

20 May

ONE OF MY MEN KILLED?

This evening, just before dusk, the colonel hurriedly started gathering up most of the B-Team to form a convoy. Word had just come from the spotter plane that four kilometers down the river there was a boat that was shot up in the water with three bodies inside. There was a peculiar mood present, with the sensation of death, the rush to get going and the possibility of further ambush awaiting. The CIDG weren't willing to go along, so the B-Team went alone in the hope of finding someone alive. McCurley was down at Ap Bac and we were worried that he might very well be on that boat. No one was found alive. The dead were Jamie Sandiecky, one of the Philippino USAID men here, Lieutenant Baker and three Vietnamese. I had known Jamie S. for the entire time

I've been here. I had met Lieutenant Baker only briefly. Ruben Delgado, the other USAID representative, was understandably shaken.

22 May

The VN outpatient people have taken off for a vacation leaving me with the whole job. This a.m. I saw 111 outpatients and this afternoon, 62. I suppose they're teaching me a good lesson. (After about a week they came back and we started working together with me trying to teach them some things.)

25 May

I am in Saigon at the USAID guest house at 9-C Tran Van Dieu. In two days Jackson and I are going to Bangkok for five days. Jackson and I came in yesterday. We flew to Can Tho first in a small spotter plane. We stopped off and saw Drs. Douglass and Marsh at the Region 2 Public Health offices. We then took a Caribou to Tan Son Nhut. We checked on our orders and I was told that I was going back about July 1 and that I would be discharged at that time, one month early, which is great. Jackson met a former schoolmate of his from Lubbock, Texas at the Hoa Loo Hotel dining room and I met a Dr. John R. who had gone to medical school with me. They had been stationed at Bong Son in II Corps, also with a MILPHAP team. Their team had been split and their five-man contingent was stationed in a dispensary at Bong Son. They were able to do some surgery, but had no operating room, only an operating table and light and a small amount of instruments. Their supply problems were worse than ours. They were often out of even local anesthetics and did some surgery without anesthesia. The First Air Cavalry was stationed only several miles from their location. They saw a total of 50 patients each day in the dispensary. Each of the two M.D.'s saw only about 15 apiece, quite a bit slower than our location. The CIDG there were Montagnards (a mountain people of different ethnic group from the Vietnamese) and didn't give the local people any problems. The local action sounded similar to that in our province.

Today I spent most of the time sitting in the Hoa Loo restaurant with Jackson and his friend Tucker who was the lab technician with the Bong Son team.

CON SON ISLAND

At one time on a Saturday I had gone to Can Tho to see Douglass about certain matters. I was unable to get a plane back until the next day and was invited to go on a side trip to Con Son Island. There were Douglass and several others, a few nurses and another MILPHAP M.D. whose team had come over on the same plane with our team. We spent a little time at the beach where fishermen were netting two-foot long, needle-nosed fish. The place looked like a likely spot for sharks so I didn't try swimming. At one point some of us got into a challenge race to the end of the runway. We ran down the sand-strewn, brush-lined runway, off the end of it and on through quite a few sand dunes to the edge of the water and then back. The footing on the dunes was soft, and we tripped a lot and fell sporadically going through them and had a good laugh at each other's apparent clumsiness. Some distance to the west of the runway supposedly were prison cells dug into the ground with bars on the top. It was rumored that some political prisoners were held there.

2 June

BANGKOK

Tomorrow Jackson and I will have to leave Bangkok and return to Vietnam. It has been a pleasant stay. The second morning here I visited three wats (Buddhist temples). One held a huge solid gold statue [96-b]. This I was told had been discovered only ten years ago. Two-hundred years ago it had been covered with a cement coat to hide its value from the invading Burmese, who would have carried it to Burma had they been aware of its value. Another wat [96-a] contained the huge reclining Buddha. It is said that the Buddha reclined in this position before his death. He is shown lying on his side with the head and chest elevated. From this I would think that Buddha died of heart failure.

One evening we spent watching Thai boxing. In addition to punching with the hands, they kick with the feet and can employ the elbows. About 15 R&R people saw the boxing that night. The tour guide was a jovial ex-boxer who seemed a bit punch drunk. He told how the Thai boxer could defeat any other combatant sport professional, such as a wrestler, conventional boxer, or karate expert. He told how contests between the Thai boxer and the others had come out with the Thai boxer the winner.

The main event was interesting. The contestants were an older man (I found this out later) and a flashy younger man. The younger went through elaborate pre-fight contortions while the older man performed but very simple homage to the gods or whatever it is they do before the fight. When the fight began, the older seemed to me to hold the upper hand for the first three rounds. In the fourth round, he was hit lightly and knocked off balance and went down. The referee came between them (it's legal to hit the other man when he's down if the referee doesn't interfere) but, the younger man gave a terrifically swift kick to the side of the older man's head and knocked him out cold; he was carried out. The older man was declared the winner because of the untimely kick. Of the eight bouts, three or four were knockouts with two contestants having to be carried out. Most of the other bouts were technical knockouts where it was apparent that the other man was helpless. The bouts were five rounds, though most lasted only two or three.

The city is not as modern as Hong Kong and some of the shops are not unlike those in Saigon, but the people and streets are clean and orderly. The people are very pleasant. I bought a few rings, one of which was called a princess ring. It had small semi-precious stones arranged in a pyramid shape, I suppose to resemble a temple. In one shop I was surprised to see for sale the skin of what must have been a rather scrawny tiger.

Back to Vietnam.

8 June

Well, I'm back in Moc Hoa again. Two nights ago the town was mortared and a company of CIDG about three miles away was overrun. I was the first one in the room to get up and let the others know that the explosions were not the 105's, but were incoming mortar rounds. Soon we were called to the hospital, and there we found about 30 casualties, as usual, accompanied by a whole host of relatives and onlookers. Things went much smoother than the last time when we had 70 and we triaged these quite speedily. We were up the whole night working on them and were quite groggy by 9 p.m. of the next day when we finally had time to rest.

Today they're having an operation. We've had two casualties come in. A helicopter that went in to get two more was just shot down.

Our new quarters have been completed and we have moved in. After a year of waiting it's finally been built. It is light-wood framed, with a high ceiling, large screens and elevated bunks (I suppose in case of floods). Thus, it was nicely designed for the tropics, that is, if one didn't have to contend with mortar shells. So, I'm not as safe here as in the old quarters, because I'm way up in the air in a top bunk. But, I'm getting good at telling what are incoming mortar rounds, and so can get down in a hurry if need be, as long as the first round doesn't land right on top of us.

10 June

Dr. Ting told me today that he had information that the VC were going to massively mortar Moc Hoa and then try to overrun it. He said there were some fresh units in Cambodia. My time left here is getting too short for something like that to happen.

12 June

A helicopter crashed a few days ago, just north of town. It had four U.S. personnel, including a colonel from the Special Forces' D-Detachment in Can Tho. None were killed. The chopper that picked them up flew them directly to Saigon without stopping at our hospital.

In Ap Bac an RF soldier didn't like the medicine he received for his cough from one of my hamlet health workers. He told the worker he wanted a shot of streptomycin. The worker told him he could not give that to him so he slugged the male worker and tore the necklace off the female worker. Higgins took the worker to the district headquarters. The district chief was not there, and he received rough handling there. Today they threw the RF into jail. I pulled the two workers out and will send two different ones if the situation straightens out.

There's machine-gun fire near the river. I hope another attack isn't about to break loose. They called an alert. I don't know if any rounds landed in town or not. Anyway, there were no casualties.

Sunday 17 June

ONE-EYED BIRD

Dr. Ruppert, Dr. Eggerstedt and I went to watch the local cockfights today at 10 a.m. They were held about four blocks away from the compound in back of a home. There were about 30 or 40 children and about the same number of adults. One of the roosters had won three previous fights and had lost one eye. He was up against another who had never been entered in a fight. The owners were betting ten dollars. I took a few photos. This was the first cockfight I'd seen. The owners prepared the roosters just like the trainers do a prize fighter. They drank from a soda bottle and spewed the water over the bird, then they poured water on a rag and drained some into the bird's mouth. The claws were laboriously sharpened. After about 20 minutes of fighting, the one-eyed bird had had enough and jumped out of the ring. This ended the fight — quite interesting.

(The thought just struck me. The U.S. was like the one-eyed bird. We had to fight the enemy on his terms. He was hidden among the populace and hard to find, while we were good targets. We were not allowed through political decisions to invade the North, which to the minds of many, would have effected a quick end to the war. The North Vietnamese-VC propaganda and terrorism were effective among the peasants, while at the same time, the propaganda at home severely undermined the efforts of our troops. We had been put in the ring to fight, with one eye, against a foe with no such impediment.)

THE OUTCOME

The ultimate outcome of this situation was the enforced subjugation of those who had been friendly to us to an unwanted Communism or vindictive retribution and the wrenching of countless others from their homeland. A further outcome with its relevance to the future was the emboldenment of the Leninist revolutionaries throughout the world and particularly in the Philippines and Central America.

Sunday 17 June continued

Yesterday a party was held by the hospital personnel for our team at the compound club. The dinner was quite good. We called in the five members of the team who were out in the district dispensaries. I had told the men not to let anyone else, particularly the Vietnamese, know we were leaving because of concern that this might have increased the danger for us. However, they must have had some idea that this was in the works.

Choppers coming in.

19 June [96-c, d]

FAREWELL

Today we leave.

The word is that there are 105mm howitzers in Cambodia aimed at us. Our two howitzers in town just let loose a barrage at something. It was unusual for them to be shooting this time of the day. Could they have been saluting us on our departure?

I said some hasty good-bys at the hospital. Ting went out with me to the runway and we shook hands. I walked over to the helicopter where there was a small group boarding in front of me. The rotors were whirling, making it impossible to communicate further. Ting was 50 yards away, standing by his jeep looking my direction. We both just stood there staring at each other for several minutes. We knew it was very possible this would be the last we would ever see of each other.

(This indeed was the last I have ever seen of them. I contacted the Red Cross to see if any of them were refugees shortly after the fall of Vietnam. I did not wish to write letters in order to avoid possible reprisal against them. Ting, Song, Nguyen, Fong — you and I know who you are. You have been some of the best friends that I have ever had. If you read this, you must contact me.)

I got into Saigon from Moc Hoa as required two days ahead of my flight back to the U.S.A. I checked at the Koepler compound where we had entered country and was told there was no room and that I would have to get a place to stay in one of the civilian hotels. First, I had to go to a downtown hotel to make arrangements to be paid for this later. I had the choice of waiting on a street corner for the Navy bus which would take an hour, or get a civilian cab. Now I'm in a captain's uniform, and two days earlier a woman sharpshooter on the back of a motorcycle had shot a lieutenant in front of the Victoria Hotel, and she was still on the loose. Well, I went to the hotel and registered and then was given a list of civilian hotels to choose from. I picked the Saigon Hotel because most of the men on the team were already there and it was only three blocks from the Koepler where I would process out. So I took a cab to the Saigon Hotel. There were no guards and all noted that I was a captain. It was a shoddy way to be pushed around, I felt, two days before being ready to go back to the States, making an easy target out of me for any interested terrorist. (A week later, ten U.S. personnel in Saigon were victims of terrorist activity in response to a visit by McNamara.)

On the last day there was a prolonged wait at Tan Son Nhut in several interconnected, small, boarded sheds without windows. It was a hot, sweaty wait. I was separated now from the rest of the men. Except for Higgins, who had stayed on, all of the men who had originally come over in the unit, were headed back home. We had given it our best effort and none of our men had been killed. So this was a goal that I'd hoped for that had been realized.

Finally, I boarded the plane. It was a Continental Boeing 707. The trip back was much more pleasant than the trip over. We were diverted north because of a storm over Hawaii. The mountain scenery coming in over Alaska was fabulous. At the Anchorage airport I bought some presents during the hour layover, and then it was on to San Francisco.

On flying low, approaching the San Francisco airport, I was struck by the sight of the freeways with their busy traffic. They seemed to be a modern insanity. The urban hassle was by now foreign to me and I didn't relish coming back to it. Moc Hoa had had the nicety of an outdoor ambulatory society — unencumbered by the automobile. When there wasn't any action going on, Moc Hoa may have had a pace and flavor akin to that of an Old West town. So coming back was like re-entry from another century and indeed from another world.

At the San Francisco airport there was more out-processing and I received my final military pay. There were some there who were telling people to resign their commissions. They said there was talk of a need for redrafting those who had recently finished their tours. I thought this sounded farfetched but wasn't absolutely sure that it wasn't true. At the time I thought these were fellow outprocessing servicemen saying these things. Later it was obvious that these were protesters who had infiltrated the area.

I wound up paying an exhorbitant fee for a cab to transfer to another airport in time so as not to miss the next flight to Milwaukee.

I really should have gone back to Medical Field Service School in San Antonio. Before we left for Vietnam, they said we should try to come back and give them a briefing on our experiences. Actually, the Army should have scheduled this before my discharge. Now, in order to do this, I would have to do it on my own. (I did not go there, but to this day I wish that I had and would have been able to relate my experiences to them.)

HOME

I got into Milwaukee at 1:30 a.m., July 2. My daughter, Jodi, age three, didn't know me and wouldn't let me pick her up for a while. The next day, she and I got along fine. It took my daughter, Heidi, a few days longer to get used to me. Heidi was eight months old. My wife and parents hadn't seemed to have changed a bit.

After being home a few days, my wife Bonnie asked me what I missed most about Vietnam. I said that I missed my mosquito net. She thought I had said that I missed ''Miss Quitoenet'' and started to get upset. It took some hurried explaining, but soon I got her to calm down and then we had a good laugh.

Soon I was immersed in the concerns of a busy pediatric residency. The thoughts of Vietnam and Moc Hoa began to fade and take a back seat to matters of the present.

BEFORE TET

I got some letters from Eggerstedt. The day after I left, they had 30 dead CIDG and seven wounded flown in and boated in from an operation they were having near My An. They ran out of body bags and had to leave the bodies on the outside for two days until choppers finally came in. After I left, Dr. E. received some temporary help from an Air Force M.D. The hospital was running quite short of medicine. Two of the girls we trained and sent to Ap Bac ran away with two RF soldiers, and there was no one left in Ap Bac except one of our men. Higgins was back at the hospital and Dr. E. assigned him as the immunization program director both in Moc Hoa and the districts. The VN outpatient health workers were giving Dr. E. a hard time. In the afternoon they would send him 90 percent of the patients while they would fiddle around with nothing important. Dr. E. was thinking of moving to the USAID house, however, the other night the VC opened up with machine-gun fire from across the river and blasted a group of houses, one of which was USAID.

Some time after I left, Ting obtained a position at a tuberculosis hospital in Saigon. One of the local VN hospital personnel was assigned to be the administrator. He didn't get along well with the new MILPHAP team or Eggerstedt and at one point was not on speaking terms with the minister of health. After a while, he was transferred. The Vietnamese hospital hygiene officer, who was a married man, fell in love with nurse Co Bong and wound up committing suicide over this. Mr. Tau, from town, who I had used as an interpreter, was gone within a year into the military, as were several other Vietnamese hospital personnel whom we had known well. Within a year the military had gotten Nguyen also. Jeff Harris, the USAID representative, became disgruntled with things in Kien Tuong and left shortly after we did. The province chief also was sent elsewhere.

Those whom I knew that remained were Song, Eggerstedt and Higgins (who had re-enlisted). For a while, Higgins had been at a district clinic. A helicopter had blown off the roof of the clinic and no one would repair it. So he went on a sit-down strike for three weeks. Finally, some VN military and townspeople fixed it up for him.

There were continued problems about keeping the pay going for the hamlet health workers. The

Special Forces were hoping for other sources of payment for them, but the Ministry of Health said they didn't have enough funds.

Ruben managed to get a large outdoor communal stove constructed for the hospital. A year later he relocated to Vung Tau.

The military action slowed down some between the time I left and Tet. One time there was an attack on the river patrol unit at the edge of town. A militia man was wounded and there were seven civilian casualties, three of whom were children.

TET

On February 2, 1968 at 4:15 a.m. the VC attacked Moc Hoa. Ruben went to his bunker at the back of his trailer office. In the bunker with him were different kinds of characters, as Ruben described them, who did not instill any sense of security. One of these was called "The Cowboy," and had all sorts of weapons. Whether he had the wherewithall to use them when the time came was doubtful. Shortly, in tumbled the psychological operations man with his radio blaring, hardly recognizable with all his gear and flak jackets. Ruben wrote a letter to Eggerstedt in this bunker at the height of the offensive. At one point he said, "I can see the L-19s and Spooky shooting down, and the noise is terrific...there just was a sudden explosion...I tore my...'' In another part he wrote, "The battle was really scary as it was just like the Fourth of July, and you really couldn't tell which was a friendly or enemy by the way the bullets and tracers, mortars and what-have-you came criss-crossing." The fighting ceased about 2 p.m. and Ruben left the bunker and went to look around town. The ARVIN were capturing remnants of the attacking force as they were fleeing from Moc Hoa, hiding among the tall grasses and weeds along Route 29, just outside the police control point going to Tan Lap, south of the hospital. Dead VC were strewn all over the road and also at the end of the road coming from the side of the hospital. Ruben went to the B-Team to inquire about a fellow Philippino who had been staying at the Catholic church nearby. Five minutes after he left, some VC who had managed to climb to the top of the church steeple, shot a B-Team soldier in the forehead, seriously wounding him. Ruben was unnerved by this because he had just been a much closer target than the man who had been hit. In Moc Hoa there were 137 dead VC plus 34 captured. Injured VC were being treated at the hospital. The VC commander was badly wounded, treated and three days later flown to Can Tho.

In the province during the Tet Offensive, total civilians killed were 48 and seriously wounded also numbered 48. There were 28 soldiers killed and 26 seriously wounded. One-hundred-and-twenty houses were 50 to 100 percent destroyed. Ting's public health man suffered a broken leg. The VC had expected the people would rise up during the Tet attack and fight on their side. Instead, said Ruben, the people were angered against the VC and the attack had united them against the Communist. Afterward, townspeople, teachers and civil servants joined together to be armed, to be trained and to defend MOC HOA.

VIỆT-NAM